A Concise Description of *Jannah & Jahannam*

the Garden of Paradise and the Fire of Hell

SHAIKH ʿABD AL-QĀDIR AL-JĪLĀNĪ

A Concise Description of *Jannah & Jahannam*

the Garden of Paradise and the Fire of Hell

Excerpted from
Sufficient Provision for Seekers of the Path of Truth
(*Al-Ghunya li-Ṭālibi Ṭarīq al-Ḥaqq*)

Translated from the Arabic By MUHTAR HOLLAND

with Preface written by
Sajid Hussain

First Published in August 2010
by
Ta-Ha Publishers Ltd,
Unit 4, The Windsor Centre,
Windsor Grove, West Norwood,
London, SE27 9NT
UK
Reprinted in 2018
Website: **www.taha.co.uk**
E-mail: sales@taha.co.uk

Cover design by: Salehah Atewala
Book Design by: Shakir Abdulcadir » opensquares.co.uk

A catalogue record of this book is available from the British Library
ISBN-13: 978-1-84200-120-2

Printed and bound by: IMAK Ofset, Turkey

بِسْمِ ٱللَّهِ ٱلرَّحْمَٰنِ ٱلرَّحِيمِ

In the name of Allāh the most Gracious the most Merciful

All Praise to Allāh, the Lord of all that exists.
There is no power or strength except with Allāh.
Peace be upon Muḥammad (Allāh bless him and give him peace),
his family and companions.

This book would not have been possible
without the kind permission of the copyright owner,
Al-Baz Publishing, Inc. Special thanks go to
Ruslan Moore and Muhtar Holland.

Contents

ix Preface

1 Concerning the causes of entry into the Fire of Hell, and the causes of entry into the Garden of Paradise.

19 Concerning the nature of the Fire of Hell and what Allāh (Almighty and Glorious is He) has prepared therein for its inhabitants, and the nature of the Garden of Paradise and what Allāh (Almighty and Glorious is He) has prepared therein for its inhabitants.

55 On crossing the bridge of Hell and entering the Garden of Paradise, as explained by the Prophet (Allāh bless him and give him peace) in a traditional report that has been handed down to us on the authority of Abū Huraira (may Allāh be well pleased with him).

89 Concerning the words of Allāh (Almighty and Glorious is He), in which He has given us the following description of the people of the Garden of Paradise.

Preface

Allāh (Almighty and Glorious is He) has decreed that in the next life man will be in one of two abodes: *Jannah* (the Garden of Paradise) or *Jahannam* (the Fire of Hell). The Garden of Paradise will be the resting place of all those who believe in Allāh (Almighty and Glorious is He) and persevere in good, as well as those whom, although they have done wrong, the Prophets or *awliyāʾ* and *ṣāliḥūn* (the righteous) intercede for them and those whom Allāh (Almighty and Glorious is He) forgives out of His vast generosity. Those who did otherwise or whom Allāh (Almighty and Glorious is He) does not forgive will be cast into the Fire of Hell, and then out of His mercy and compassion, Allāh (Almighty and Glorious is He) will rescue any of the *muʾminūn* who have even an atom of *īmān* in their hearts. This essay discusses the Divine Wisdom in the creation of these two abodes.

This world is a testing ground. What happens here determines our situation in the life to come. The end of the *muḥsinūn* (people who do good), or even of penitent wrongdoers, cannot be the same as that of unrepentant *fāsiqūn* (transgressors). Were it so, it would render void the attribute of Allāh (Almighty and Glorious is He) of *ʿadālah* (justice). Those who do have *īmān* and do good must of necessity be recompensed for their *īmān* and their actions. For this, the Garden of Paradise was created. It is everything that this world is not. The life of this world, its pains and its pleasures, is nothing more than the blink of an eye; the Garden of Paradise is everlasting. This world is transient; the next, eternal. The inhabitants of the Garden shall have whatever their hearts desire. They will know no pain or grief and will receive that which no eye has seen, no ear has heard and which has never occurred to the mind of a human being. Ease and comfort is all that they will experience. This is the reward the Almighty has promised to those of His believing slaves who do good. Its reason for having been created is nothing more than to amply reward those who are successful.

Allāh (Almighty and Glorious is He) is *ar-Raḥmān* (the Beneficent) and *ar-Raḥīm* (the Merciful), but He is also *al-ʿAdl* (Justice itself). So, just as the *muḥsinūn* must be rewarded, so too must those who do evil be punished. The harm they cause to other people and to themselves cannot go unpunished unless they turn in repentance to Allāh (Almighty and Glorious is He) or unless Allāh (Almighty and Glorious is He) forgives them freely out of His vast generosity.

The Day of Judgement is also known as the Day of *Taghābun* (mutual recompense) because on that Day those who suffered at the hands of others will take from their good deeds as a form of recompense for the suffering they endured in this world. Allāh (Almighty and Glorious is He) is aware of all that unrepentant *kāfirūn* transgressors do, whether they conceal it or do it openly, and in the Hereafter He will exact retribution from them. They will be thrown on their faces into the Blazing Fire to abide therein forever. Every time they die they will be restored to life only to die again. They will know only agony. It is for this, the punishing of the *kāfirūn* (disbelievers) and *fāsiqūn*, that the Fire of Hell was created.

Allāh (Most Gracious) desires only good for his slaves. He does not wish to punish us, even though He has every right to do so. In His wisdom, He has therefore decided to convey to us some of the delights of the Garden of Paradise, so that we may be spurred on to good. The descriptions given in the Glorious Qurʾān about the Garden of Paradise are thus only that which is most beautiful and pleasing, that which would shake man from his lethargy to become of the *muḥsinūn*. Allāh (Almighty and Glorious is He) says: "**For them will be Gardens of Eternity; beneath them rivers will flow; they will be adorned therein with bracelets of gold, and they will wear green garments of fine silk and heavy brocade: They will recline therein on raised thrones. How good the recompense! How beautiful a couch to recline on!**" (Qurʾān 18:31)

It is the nature of most men that they always want something in return for anything they may have to do. The knowledge of the Garden of Paradise is thus an assurance to them that they will not go unrewarded. They engage in those deeds which are pleasing to their Lord and try to abstain from those which are displeasing to Him, so that they may acquire the good of the next world.

"The promise of Allāh is true." (Qur'ān 28:13) The believing servants know this, and when they read about what is promised to them of the pleasures of the Garden of Paradise in the Book of Allāh, it is an encouragement for them to do good. They submit themselves to Allāh (Almighty and Glorious is He), knowing that the sufferings of this world are but a trifle compared to the joys of the Garden of Paradise.

Man is in a constant battle against his own desires. It is only through *taqwā* (God-consciousness) that he is able to overcome these desires. Allāh (Almighty and Glorious is He) has therefore informed us of the chastisement of the Fire of Hell in order to strike fear into the hearts of the believers. The Fire of Hell is thus described in the most frightening terms. One example is the *āya* of Allāh (Almighty and Glorious is He): **"And beyond him is Hell where he will be given pus to drink. He gulps at it but can hardly swallow it down. Death comes at him from every side but he does not die. And beyond him is relentless punishment."** (Qur'ān 14:16-17) And there is also: **"But no! It is a Raging Blaze stripping away the limbs and scalp."** (Qur'ān 70:15-16) It is a reminder to us, when we are tempted to sin, of the consequences of that action. The fear of the anger of Allāh (Almighty and Glorious is He) thus prevents us from falling into error.

Allāh (Almighty and Glorious is He) is *al-Baṣīr* (All-Seeing) and *al-ʿAlīm* (All-Knowing). He is informed about everything which happens in the heavens and the earth. The actions of His slaves and the suffering they endure are all known to Him. He therefore says: "**Their Lord responds to them: 'I will not let the deeds of any doer among you go to waste, male or female – you are both the same in that respect. Those who emigrated and were driven from their homes and suffered harm in My Way and fought and were killed, I will erase their bad actions from them and admit them into Gardens with rivers flowing under them, as a reward from Allāh. The best of all rewards is with Allāh.'**" (Qur'ān 3:195) We learn from this *āya* that our sins will be blotted out as if they had never occurred, if only we bear with patience and fortitude the trials that active Muslims suffer in this world. We will become inhabitants of the Garden of Paradise. But the Garden of Paradise itself is not the ultimate achievement. There is a reward greater than it and that is to attain the pleasure of Allāh (Almighty and Glorious is He).

Our fate will be determined by our *īmān* and our actions. There are angels assigned to each one of us to record what we do. They know and see all our commissions and omissions and do not fail in recording them. We therefore cannot escape from Allāh (Almighty and Glorious is He). Rather we should turn to Him in repentance before death overtakes us. We should strive our utmost to be of those who will enter the Garden of Paradise and should hate to become of the inhabitants of the Fire of Hell.

Sajid Hussain

Concerning the causes of entry into the Fire of Hell, and the causes of entry into the Garden of Paradise

You should know that entry into the Fire of Hell is the result of unbelief [*kufr*] and the multiplication of punishment, and that the allotment of the descending levels [*darakāt*] is determined by the scale of evil deeds and evil traits of character. Entry into the Garden of Paradise, on the other hand, is the result of faith [*īmān*] and the multiplication of blessed grace, while the allotment of the ascending levels [*darajāt*] is determined by the scale of righteous deeds and excellent traits of character.

You must also know that Allāh (Almighty and Glorious is He) created the Garden of Paradise and filled it with blissful comfort, as a reward for those who are worthy of it, that He created the Fire of Hell and filled it with torment, as a punishment for those who deserve it, and that He created this world and filled it with disasters as well as blessings, as an ordeal and a trial. Then, when He created His human creatures, He made the Garden of Paradise and the Fire of Hell invisible to them, so that they could not see them directly with their ordinary eyes. The blessings and disasters that exist in this world are therefore meant to serve as the model [*unmūdhaj*] of the Hereafter, and as the means by which the taste of it can be experienced.

He also created kings from among His servants here on this earth, and He conferred on them an authority that would be potent enough to instil terror in people's hearts and to control their personal inclinations. This was meant to serve as a model [*unmūdhaj*] and an allegory [*mithāl*] of His planning and management, His dominion, and the effectiveness of His command and His way of dealing with things.

He therefore provided information about all of this by way of revelation [*tanzīl*]. He described the two abodes [the abode of this world and the abode of the Hereafter], and He described His dominion [*mulk*], His power [*qudra*], His planning and management [*tadbīr*], His gracious favour [*minna*], and His works [*ṣanāʾiʿ*]. For this purpose He used the technique of coining similitudes [*amthāl*], then He said (Exalted is He):

> *wa tilka ʾl-amthālu naḍribu-hā li ʾn-nāsi wa mā yaʿqilu-hā illa ʾl-ʿālimūn.*
>
> **And as for these similitudes, We coin them for mankind, but none will grasp their meaning except those who have [the necessary] knowledge. (29:43)**

Those who are well versed in the knowledge of Allāh [*al-ʿulamāʾ bi-llāh*] are therefore qualified to understand what Allāh (Almighty and Glorious is He) intends to convey by His similitudes, because a similitude is merely the depiction of something you have already witnessed with your own eyes, in order to let you see the characteristic features of that which is otherwise invisible to you. It is a device for enabling you to perceive what you cannot perceive with your ordinary eye, by causing the perceptive faculty of your heart to penetrate that which your eyesight is incapable of perceiving. Your heart can thus make sense of all the information that is being addressed to it – information about the Kingdom of Heaven [*al-Malakūt*], information about the two abodes [*ad-dārain*], and information about the King of kings [*Mālik al-mulūk*].

There is not a single delight or pleasure in this world that does not serve as a model for the Garden of Paradise, and as a foretaste of what will be experienced therein. Beyond all this, however, the Garden of Paradise also contains that which no eye has ever seen, of which no ear has ever heard, and the very notion of which has never occurred to any human heart.[1] If any element of this mystery were to be mentioned by name to the servants [of the Lord], the use of such a name would be to no avail, because they cannot understand its meaning here below, since they have never seen what it refers to, and it has no model in this world. The Garden of Paradise actually has no fewer than one hundred ascending levels [*darajāt*], but He has described only three of them: one as consisting of gold, one as consisting of silver, and one as consisting of light. Then, beyond that point, there is something incomprehensible, something which human minds are quite incapable of grasping.

As for the agony and torment that exist in this world, these likewise constitute a model, which serves to represent the abode of punishment [in the Fire of Hell]. But then again, beyond all this, there is something that human minds are quite incapable of comprehending. In this case, that something is a whole assortment of unimaginable torments.

Whatever may lie in store for those who are condemned to the Fire of Hell, it will emerge to meet them out of His wrath, and whatever may lie in store for those who are worthy of the Garden of Paradise, it will emerge to greet them out of His mercy. For each and every one of His servants who has acquired no more than his lawful share of this world, and thanked Him for it, He will provide recompense in the Garden of Paradise; a recompense so great that his share of this world will seem quite tiny by comparison. By acquiring things that were not lawful to him, on the other hand, a person

1 An allusion to the Divine Saying [*Ḥadīth Qudsī*]: I have prepared for My righteous servants that which no eye has ever seen, of which no ear has ever heard, and the very notion of which has never occurred to any human heart.

will deprive himself of his portion of the ascending levels [*darajāt*], and anyone who denies their very existence will be utterly deprived of the Garden of Paradise and all that it contains.

For those who are worthy to inhabit the Garden of Paradise, there will be brides [*ʿarāʾis*] and wedding feasts [*walāʾim*] and hospitable entertainments [*ḍiyāfāt*]. The brides are for the benefit of the single men [*diʿwa*], for the very good reason that the Lord of Honour [*Rabb al-ʿIzza*] (Glory be to Him) has summoned them to the Abode of Peace [*Dār as-Salām*] in order that He may provide them with fresh new bodies and everlasting lives. The wedding feasts are for the benefit of the married partners, and the hospitable entertainments are for the receptions of guests – to provide opportunities for the inhabitants of the Garden of Paradise to meet with one another, to exchange visits, and to converse in settings of intimate conviviality. They will have a gathering place in the shade of the Tree of Bliss [*Ṭūbā*],[2] where they will meet the Messengers [*Rusul*] and visit with them, as well as enjoying occasional sessions in the company of the angels (may the peace of Allāh be upon them all).

Other amenities available to them will include market places, where they can come and select various shapes and forms, and gifts from the All-Merciful [*ar-Raḥmān*] at the times of the ritual prayers [*ṣalawāt*]. They will have all kinds of food, drink and fruits at their disposal at every moment of the day, be it early in the morning or late at night. Their various forms of nourishment will actually be a constantly flowing stream, never cut off and never interrupted. They will receive an increase from Allāh (Almighty and Glorious is He) with every day that passes, and as soon as they receive the latest increment, they will forget what they had before.

---

2 The *Ṭūbā* tree is traditionally depicted as having its root in Paradise, while its leaves and branches extend downwards towards the earth. According to some accounts, one of its branches will enter the mansion of each inhabitant of the Garden of Paradise, bearing flowers and ripe fruit of every imaginable kind.

Then there is a park or recreation ground [*muntazah*] for them to enjoy. They will find it situated in the midst of charming meadows on the bank of the River of Abundance [*al-Kawthar*].[3] Pitched on the grounds of that park are pavilions made of pearls. Each pavilion is sixty miles in length and an equal distance in width, and is made of one single pearl [*lu'lu'a*] in which no hole has been pierced. Inside those pavilions there are maidservants fragrantly perfumed, who have never been looked at by an angel, nor by any of the people of the Garden of Paradise, such as the attendants and the houries [*ḥūr*]. We know about them from the words of Allāh (Almighty and Glorious is He):

> *fī-hinna khairātun ḥisān.*
> **In them [are maidens] good and beautiful. (55:70)**

Since Allāh (Almighty and Glorious is He) calls them beautiful [*ḥisān*], who else could even attempt to describe their beauty [*ḥusn*]?! Then He goes on to say (Exalted is He):

> *ḥūrun maqṣūrātun fi 'l-khiyām.*
> **Fair ones, cloistered in pavilions. (55:72)**

For they are the select choice of the All-Merciful One [*ar-Raḥmān*], who has chosen their beautiful forms out of all the forms in existence. They have been created from the clouds of His mercy [*raḥma*], for when those clouds deliver rain, they send forth a shower of beautiful maidservants, in compliance with the wish of the All-Generous One [*al-Karīm*]. The light of their faces comes from the light of the Heavenly Throne [*'Arsh*]. Pavilions of pearl have been pitched over them, so no one has seen them since the

---

3 Shaikh 'Abd al-Qādir al-Jīlānī (may Allāh be well pleased with him) tells us that, according to the tradition [*ḥadīth*] of Anas ibn Mālik (may Allāh be well pleased with him), Allāh's Messenger (Allāh bless him and give him peace) once said: I was admitted to the Garden of Paradise, and – lo and behold! – there I was beside a flowing stream, flanked on both sides by pavilions made of pearls. I dipped my hand in [what looked like] water flowing by, and – lo and behold! – it was musk, of the most exquisitely fragrant kind. I said "O Gabriel, what is this?" He replied: "This is the River of Abundance [*al-Kawthar*], which Allāh (Exalted is He) has bestowed upon you."

moment of their creation, for they are "cloistered in pavilions [*maqṣūrātun fi'l-khiyām*]." To say that they have been cloistered [*quṣirna*] is a way saying that they have been kept in confinement, so as to be accessible to their husbands alone, and to no one else in the whole of creation.

The inhabitants of the Garden of Paradise will thus lead a life of ease and comfort within palatial mansions [*quṣūr*] and in the company of their spouses. They will tarry in this state of blissful happiness as long as Allāh (Almighty and Glorious is He) wills it so – until the day comes when Allāh (Almighty and Glorious is He) wishes to introduce them to a new kind of bliss [*niʿma*] and a new form of recreation [*nuzha*], at which point they will hear a voice calling out to them on all the ascending levels of the Gardens of Paradise [*darajāt al-Jinān*]: "O people of the Gardens of Paradise, this is the day of entertainment and happiness, relaxation and joy. You must therefore go out to your recreation ground [*muntazah*]."

In response to this call, they will sally forth on horses of pearl and sapphire, riding like the lords of their cities as they head out towards those open spaces. Then they will travel over those open spaces to those charming meadows on the bank of the River of Abundance [*al-Kawthar*], and so Allāh (Almighty and Glorious is He) will guide them to their camp sites. Every man amongst them will then dismount beside his pavilion - only to find that there is no entrance to it. The pavilion must therefore be penetrated by some means other than an ordinary doorway, and this is done when it is split open by the eye of the saintly friend [*walī*] of Allāh (Exalted is He), in order to let him know that she who is inside the pavilion has never been examined by anyone else – in fulfilment of the promise previously given by Allāh (Almighty and Glorious is He), in the abode of this world, in as much as He said:

fī-hinna khairātun ḥisān.

In them [are maidens] good and beautiful. (55:70)

And then He said (Exalted is He):

ḥūrun maqṣūrātun fī 'l-khiyām.

Fair ones, cloistered in pavilions. (55:72)

And then He went on to say:

lam yaṭmith-hunna insun qabla-hum wa-lā jānn.

[Fair ones] whom neither man nor Jinn will have touched before them. (55:74)

The man then will recline beside her on the couch of recreation [*sarīr an-nuzha*] inside those curtained canopies [*ḥijāl*]. Like each of the other men, he will be treated to a portion of her nuptial banquet [*walīma*]. Then, when they have sampled the main courses of the nuptial banquets, Allāh (Almighty and Glorious is He) will provide them with pure wine to quench their thirst. They will derive great pleasure from the novel fruits with which Allāh (Almighty and Glorious is He) supplies them on that day – from all those novel gifts, including the decorations [*ḥulā*] and the suits of clothes [*ḥulal*], for they will be invested with the raiment of the All-Mighty One [*kiswat ar-Raḥmān*]. They will busy themselves with the maidens good and beautiful, who will satisfy their every wish and desire. Then they will move on to enjoy the delights of sitting on the marvellous carpets [*ʿabqariyyāt*], embroidered with all kinds of decorative patterns, that grace the banks of the streams in those charming meadows. They will climb aboard the green cradle-cushions [*rafārif*] and recline upon them in comfort. All of this is foretold in His words (Exalted is He):

muttakiʾīna ʿalā rafrafin khuḍrin wa ʿabqariyyin ḥisān.

[There they will be] reclining on green cradle-cushions and beautiful rugs. (55:76)

When Allāh (Almighty and Glorious is He) calls something beautiful, what is left for anyone else to say about it? As for the cradle-cushion [*rafraf*], it is something that causes a person who reclines upon it to rock to and fro – as on a swing [*urjūḥa*] – to right and left, and up and down, while sharing the fun of the ride with his close companion.

When they climb aboard the cradle-cushions, Isrāfīl[4] (peace be upon him) will break into song. According to the traditional report [*khabar*] that has been handed down to us:[5]

> Of all the creatures of Allāh (Exalted is He), not one has a voice more beautiful than that of Isrāfīl (peace be upon him). So, when he breaks into song, the inhabitants of the seven heavens have their ritual prayer (*ṣalāt*) and their glorification (*tasbīḥ*) cut short.

When they climb aboard the cradle-cushions and Isrāfīl starts singing all kinds of songs, hymning the glory and the holiness of the King Most Holy [*al-Mālik al-Quddūs*], not a single tree in the Garden of Paradise will fail to blossom, not a single screen or door will fail to tremble and burst open, not a single doorbell will fail to tinkle with its full array of chimes, and not a single thicket of gold and silver canes will fail to let the sound of his voice blow through its reeds. Those reeds will therefore play all kinds of tunes. Among all the maidens with eyes so fair [*al-ḥūr al-ʿīn*][6] not a single one will fail to sing her songs, and the birds will join in with their melodies.

---

4 Isrāfīl (peace be upon him) is the angel who is charged with the task of sounding the trumpet on the Day of Resurrection.

5 As used by the relaters of tradition, the term *khabar* is sometimes synonymous with *ḥadīth*, meaning a report that can be traced all the way back to the Prophet Muḥammad himself (Allāh bless him and give him peace), whether the substance of that report be a saying of his or a description of his behaviour in a certain situation. In some cases, however, the term *khabar* is applied to a tradition that may well have been originated with the Prophet (Allāh bless him and give him peace), but which can only be traced with certainty to one of his Companions, or to some other reliable early source.

6 In other words, the "houries" of Paradise, mentioned several times in the Qurʾān. Literally, according to the Arabic lexicographers, "women whose eyes are characterised by intense whiteness of the part that is white, and intense blackness of the part that is black," or, more poetically, "women with eyes resembling a gazelle." Pickthall translates *wa zawwajnāhum bi-ḥūrin ʿīn* (Qurʾān 44:54): **"And We shall wed them unto fair ones with wide, lovely eyes."** (See: *The Glorious Koran*. English translation by Muḥammad Marmaduke Pickthall. London: George Allen & Unwin, 1980)

Allāh (Almighty and Glorious is He) will then tell the angels by way of inspiration: "Respond to them, and let the sound of your voices be heard by those servants of Mine who have kept their choral music [*samā*ʿ] free from contamination by the woodwind instruments of Satan [*mazāmīr ash-Shaiṭān*]." The angels will promptly respond with melodies and sounds of a spiritual nature [*rūḥaniyya*]. These sounds will blend together, so as to become a single vibration. At this point Allāh (Exalted is He) will say: "Arise, O David, and stand by the leg of My Throne, then celebrate My Glory!" David will launch at once into the celebration of His Glory, using a voice that overflows all other voices and makes them sound much sweeter.

The pleasure experienced by the people of the pavilions will thus be multiplied again and again, as they rock to and fro and swing up and down on those cradle-cushions for they will be surrounded by all kinds of delightful sensations and songs. All of this is foretold in His words (Almighty and Glorious is He):

> *[fa-amma 'lladhīna āmanū wa ʿamilu 'ṣ-ṣāliḥāti] fa-hum fī rawḍatin yuḥbarūn.*
>
> **[As for those who believed, and did good works], they shall be made happy in a charming meadow. (30:15)**

It was Yaḥyā ibn Kathīr[7] (may Allāh bestow His mercy upon him) who said [in commenting on this particular Qur'ānic verse]: "The 'charming meadow' [*ar-rawḍa*] means sensual pleasures and musical entertainment [*al-ladhdha wa 's-samā*ʿ]."

7 Abū Zakariyā' Yaḥyā ibn Hishām ibn Kathīr ibn Qais al-Ghassānī (may Allāh bestow His mercy upon him) was an expert in the tradition of the Prophet (Allāh bless him and give him peace), although some authorities have questioned his reliability. The date of his death has not been recorded, but he is known to have been a student of al-Aʿmash (d. ca. 148) and other traditionists of the same period.

Suddenly, while they are busily indulging in their sensual pleasures and enjoying their merry delight, the gateway of the King Most Holy [*al-Mālik al-Quddūs*] – that is to say, the gateway of the Garden of Eden [*Jannat ʿAdn*] – will open unto them. The sound of the voices of spiritual beings [*rūḥānniyyīn*], arrayed in ranks, will then issue forth from the Garden of Eden, vibrantly hymning the praises of the All-Generous and Nobly Exalted One [*tamājīd al-Mājid al-Karīm*] to all the ascending levels of the Gardens of Paradise [*darajāt al-Jinān*]. A wind of Eden will begin to blow, wafting forth all kinds of sweet perfume, spreading the breath of life, and fanning the gentle breeze [*nasīm*] – that is to say, the gentle breeze of nearness [to the Lord].

In the wake of this, a light will shine, and its radiance will shed a brilliant glow upon charming meadows, their pavilions, and the banks of their rivers and streams. Every single thing that belongs to them will be filled with light. Then the Majestic One (Magnificent is His Majesty) [*al-Jalīl – jalla Jalālu-hu*] will call out to them from up above their heads:

"Peace be upon you [*as-salāmu ʿalaikum*], My dear ones [*aḥibbāʾī*], My saintly friends [*awliyāʾī*] and My chosen ones [*aṣfiyāʾī*]! O people of the Garden of Paradise, how did you find your recreational park [*muntazah*]? This is your special day, in lieu of the New Year's Day [*Nairūz*] of My enemies. They tried to find a special day in the world below, in order to freshen and renew for themselves the blissful happiness which they had spoiled for themselves on account of their wicked conduct and their wretched behaviour. But they failed to obtain the pleasure they were seeking.

"They incurred nothing but loss, instead of what they sought to acquire immediately, in the temporal realm [*fi 'l-ʿājil*], and they were too impatient to wait until they could obtain all this, which I had prepared in the realm of the future [*fi 'l-ājil*], for the benefit of those who were faithfully committed to obeying Me. You turned your backs on all that they found so intensely interesting, and you refused to get involved in matters that stir up rivalry and mutual competition among people addicted to the lower world. Ah well, today they are tasting the evil consequences of that which spurred them to compete with one another in such pointless rivalry.

"How swiftly it all came to a sudden end – the sensual pleasure and the greedy satisfaction they sought in the abode of fleeting existence [*dār al-fanā'*]! They have been reduced to humiliation and disgrace, whereas you have been rewarded for your patience with a Garden of Paradise, with garments of silk, with a park for recreation, and with a greeting of 'Peace!' This day is indeed your New Year's Day [*Nairūz*] and your opportunity for happy relaxation. This day is the occasion of your visit to My Abode [*Dārī*] in the Garden of Eden.

"How often I saw you during the days of your lives in the world below, on the likes of this day, busily engaged in My worship and in faithful obedience to Me! They would be luxuriating in their idle sport and games – intoxicated, bewildered, sinfully disobedient and rebellious. They would be enjoying the ephemeral vanities of the lower world, and gleefully rejoicing in the way those vanities rotated and circulated amongst them, whereas you would be vigilantly devoted to the contemplation of My Majesty [*Jalāl*], keeping strictly within the limits set by My rules of law [*ḥudūd*], observing the terms of My covenant [*'ahd*], and taking the utmost care to respect My rights [*ḥuqūq*]."

At this point, one of the doors of the Fires of Hell will be held open for the benefit of the inhabitants of the Gardens of Paradise. As the flames and the smoke belch forth, along with the screams and the yelling and howling of the people inside, they will view the scene from those comfortable seats of theirs. They will recognise and appreciate how bountiful are the favours that Allāh (Almighty and Glorious is He) has bestowed upon them, and so they will experience an even greater measure of exultation and happiness.

As for the inhabitants of the Fire of Hell, they will gaze out from those jails and prison cells, shackled by those fetters and chains, and they will feel bitter disappointment over what has passed them by. They will stare at the faces of the inhabitants of the Gardens of Paradise, desperately imploring them to appeal on their behalf for Allāh's help, and calling out to them by their personal names, so Allāh (Blessed is His Name) will say:

> *inna aṣḥāba 'l-jannati 'l-yawma fī shughulin fākihūn: hum wa azwāju-hum fī ẓilālin ʿala 'l-arāʾiki muttakiʾūn: la-hum fī-hā fākihatun wa la-hum mā yaddaʿūn salām: qawlan min Rabbin Raḥīm wa 'mtāzu 'l-yawma ayyuha 'l-mujrimūn: a-lam aʿhad ilai-kum yā Banī Ādama al-lā taʿbudu 'sh-shaiṭān inna-hu lakum ʿaduwwun mubīn: wa ani 'ʿbudūnī: hādhā ṣirāṭun mustaqīm.*
>
> **See, those who are worthy of the Garden [of Paradise] are busy this day in their rejoicing, they and their spouses, reclining upon couches in the shade. There they have fruits, and they have all that they call for. "Peace!" – such is the greeting from a Lord All-Compassionate. But keep yourselves apart, O you guilty ones, on this day. Did I not make a covenant with you, O you sons of Adam, that you should not worship Satan – surely he is an obvious enemy to you – and that you should worship Me? This is a straight path. (36:55-61)**

The Fire of Hell will therefore blaze all the more fiercely for them, and so their gathered throng will be dispersed and their plaintive wailing will cease. They will then be tossed towards islands in the Fire of Hell, and there, as soon as they have scrambled ashore, scorpions with stings as big as date palms will come crawling to meet them. The next thing to come rushing towards them will be a torrential stream of fire, fuelled by the wrath of the All-Compelling One [*al-Jabbār*]. This flood will sweep them away and plunge them deep into the oceans of the Fires of Hell, and a herald will proclaim at the behest of Allāh (Exalted is He):

"This is your special day, the one you have been provoking Me to prepare for you by committing monstrous sins, by rebelling against Me in spite of My bountiful blessings, and by taking such gleeful delight – while still in the abode of sorrows and servitude – in what you dared to consider comparable to that which I have prepared for people faithfully committed to obeying Me. Well, those sensual pleasures are over and done with, as far as you are concerned, so now you must taste the evil consequences of the course you preferred to adopt.

"Those who have proved themselves worthy of the Garden of Paradise – from whose number you are totally excluded – are the ones who are now busily engaged in the luxurious enjoyment of wedding banquets, all kinds of fruits and an exquisite variety of gifts, the deflowering of virgin brides, the thrill of riding on the cradle-cushions [*rafārif*], the sweet delight of listening to songs and many different types of music, My greeting of peace upon them, My kind and gentle treatment of them, and then in addition to all this, something designed to exhaust all their previous blessings, in order to make them ready to experience their state of bliss anew, and to receive a pleasure that will greatly exceed the pleasure they have already enjoyed.

"O you who have proved yourselves worthy of the Garden of Paradise, this day has been granted to you, instead of the day of My enemies, who greeted one another [on their New Year's Day], and gave gifts to their kings and accepted gifts from them. You are the triumphantly successful ones [*al-fā'izūn*]!"[8]

---

8 This is an obvious allusion to the verse [*āya*] of the Qur'ān in which Allāh (Almighty and Glorious is He) has told us: *lā yastawī aṣḥābu 'n-nāri wa aṣḥābu 'l-janna: aṣḥābu 'l-jannati humu 'l-fā'izūn.* **Not equal are the inhabitants of the Fire of Hell and the inhabitants of the Garden of Paradise. The inhabitants of the Garden of Paradise – they are the triumphantly successful ones! (59:20)**

Abū Huraira[9] (may Allāh be well pleased with him) is reported as having said: "A man once said to Allāh's Messenger (Allāh bless him and give him peace): 'I happen to be a man who is very fond of the sound of a beautiful voice, so tell me, is the sound of a beautiful voice to be heard in the Garden of Paradise?' He responded to this (may Allāh be well pleased with him) by saying: 'Yes indeed, by Him in whose Hand is my soul! By way of inspiration, Allāh (Almighty and Glorious as He) will instruct a tree in the Garden of Paradise to declare on his behalf: 'Listen to this, O My servants, who have been too preoccupied with My worship and My remembrance to indulge in making music with guitars [*barābiṭ*] and woodwind instruments [*mazāmīr*]!' The tree will then raise its voice to a higher pitch, producing a sound the likes of which no beings in the world of creation have ever heard before, in order to hymn the glory of the Lord and to celebrate His holiness."

Abū Qallāba (may Allāh bestow His mercy upon him) is reported as having said: "A man once said to Allāh's Messenger (Allāh bless him and give him peace): 'Is there such a thing as night in the Garden of Paradise?' He responded to this (may Allāh be well pleased with him) by saying: 'Whatever can have prompted you to ask that question?' The man then said: 'I heard the statement made by Allāh (Almighty and Glorious is He) in His Book:

> *wa la-hum rizqu-hum fī-hā bukratan wa ʿashiyyā.*
>
> **And in it they shall have their sustenance, in the early morning and in the evening. (19:62)**

– so I said to myself: "Night in the Garden of Paradise must fall between the early morning and the evening time."' But Allāh's Messenger (Allāh bless him and give him peace) told him: 'There is no night over there.

9 Abū Huraira ["Father of a Kitten"] is a nickname he acquired on account of his fondness for a little cat. His real name is uncertain, although some call him Abū Huraira ad-Dawsī al-Yamānī. He is famous for having related more traditions than any other Companion of the Prophet (Allāh bless him and give him peace). Having embraced Islām in A.H. 7, the year of the expedition to Khaibar, he joined the special group of materially impoverished Muslims known as the Companions of the Bench [*Aṣḥāb aṣ-Ṣuffa*]. He died in Medina in A.H. 57 or 59, at the age of 78.

There is never anything other than radiance and light. The forenoon [*ghuduww*] turns into the afternoon [*rawāḥ*], and then the afternoon turns directly into the next forenoon. The inhabitants receive an exquisite variety of gifts from Allāh (Almighty and Glorious is He), at the times prescribed for the ritual prayers [*ṣalawāt*] which they used to perform in the lower world, and the angels salute them with the greeting of peace.'"

For anyone who wishes to enjoy a share in this delightful and everlasting life, it is essential to observe with care the rules and conditions of true devotion [*taqwā*], as they are set forth in His words (Almighty and Glorious is He):

> *laisa 'l-birra an tuwallū wujūha-kum qibala 'l-mashriqi wa 'l-maghribi wa lakinna 'l-birra man āmana bi-'llāhi wa 'l-yawmi 'l-ākhiri wa 'l-malā'ikati wa 'l-kitābi wa 'n-nabiyyīn: wa āta 'l-māla 'alā ḥubbi-hi dhawi 'l-qurbā wa 'l-yatāmā wa 'l-masākīna wa 'bna 's-sabīli wa 's-sā'ilīna wa fi 'r-riqāb: wa aqāma 'ṣ-ṣalāta wa āta 'z-zakāh: wa 'l-mūfūna bi-'ahdi-him idhā 'āhadū: wa 'ṣ-ṣābirīna fi'l-ba'sā'i wa 'ḍ-ḍarrā'i wa ḥīna 'l-ba's: ulā'ika 'lladhīna ṣadaqū: ulā'ika humu 'l-muttaqūn.*
>
> **It is not piety, that you turn your faces to the East and to the West. True piety is [the piety of] one who believes in Allāh and the Last Day and the angels and the Book and the Prophets; one who gives his wealth, for love of Him to kinsfolk and to orphans and the needy and the wayfarer and to those who beg, and to set slaves free; one who duly performs the ritual prayer, and pays the alms-due. [It is the piety of those] those who fulfil their covenant when they have committed themselves to a covenant, and who are patient in tribulation and adversity and in time of stress. Such are they who are sincere. Such are the truly devout. (2:177)**

It is also incumbent upon such a person to ensure that the prescribed penalties and reparations of Islām are duly put into effect.

Ḥudhaifa ibn al-Yamān[10] (may Allāh be well pleased with him) is reported as having said, in an interpretative commentary [*tafsīr*] on His words (Exalted is He):

> *yā ayyuha 'lladhīna āmanu 'dkhulū fi 's-silmi kāffa.*
> **O you who believe, come into [the religion of] peace, each and every one of you. (2:208):**

"Islām consists of eight portions: (1) The ritual prayer [*ṣalāt*] is a portion, (2) the alms-due [*zakāt*] is a portion, (3) fasting [*ṣiyām*] is a portion, (4) the Pilgrimage [*Ḥajj*] is a portion, (5) the Lesser Pilgrimage or Visitation [*ʿUmra*] is a portion, (6) the sacred struggle or holy war [*jihād*] is a portion, (7) enjoining what is right and fair [*al-amr bi-'l-maʿrūf*] is a portion, and (8) forbidding what is wrong and unfair [*an-nahy ʿani 'l-munkar*] is a portion.[11] What a terrible failure is he who has no portion at all!"

According to a report transmitted by ʿĀṣim, i.e., ʿĀṣim the Cross-Eyed [*al-Aḥwal*], on the authority of Anas ibn Mālik[12] (may Allāh be well pleased with him), the Prophet (Allāh bless him and give him peace) once said:

---

10 Abū Abdi'llāh Ḥudhaifa ibn [the son of] al-Yamān al-ʿAbasī (may Allāh be well pleased with them both) was among the earliest to embrace Islām, and he came to be one of the most distinguished of all the Companions of the Prophet (Allāh bless him and give him peace). He was famous for his abstinent way of life. Together with Abu 'd-Dardāʾ and Abū Dharr (may Allāh be well pleased with both of them), he was one of those Companions who were called '*ṣāḥib sirr an-Nabī*', because of the secret knowledge imparted to them by the Prophet (Allāh bless him and give him peace). He died in A.H. 36.

11 The seventh and eighth of these "portions of Islām" are of considerable importance to anyone seeking for a better understanding of the varied manifestations of "political activism" in the contemporary Muslim world.

12 Abū Hamza Anas ibn Mālik (d. A.H. 91-3) is one of the most prolific narrators of Prophetic tradition. His mother presented him as a servant to the Prophet (Allāh bless him and give him peace), in whose service he remained until his master died. Anas himself lived on to a very advanced age (according to various accounts, he was somewhere between 97 and 107 years old when he died).

The likeness of Islām is that of a firm and sturdy tree: Belief in Allāh [*al-īmān bi'llāh*] is its root. The five daily ritual prayers [*ṣalawāt*] are its forks. The fast [*ṣiyām*] of Ramadan is its bark. The Pilgrimage [*Ḥajj*] and the Visitation [*ʿUmra*] are its sap. The minor ablution [*wuḍūʾ*] and the major ablution [*ghusl*] to remove defilement are its supply of water. The reverential treatment of one's parents [*birr al-wālidain*] and respect for the bond of kinship [*ṣilat ar-raḥim*] are its branches. The scrupulous avoidance of things forbidden by Allāh [*al-kaff ʿan mahārimi 'llāh*] makes up its foliage. Righteous deeds [*aʿmāl ṣāliḥa*] are its fruit, and the remembrance of Allāh [*dhikru 'llāh*] makes up its veins.

Then he went on to say (Allāh bless him and give him peace):

Just as a tree can neither flourish nor develop properly unless it bears green leaves, Islām cannot develop properly except through the scrupulous avoidance of things forbidden by Allāh (Almighty and Glorious is He) , and through the doing of righteous deeds.

Concerning the nature of the Fire of Hell and what Allāh (Almighty and Glorious is He) has prepared therein for its inhabitants, and the nature of the Garden of Paradise and what Allāh (Almighty and Glorious is He) has prepared therein for its inhabitants

Abū Huraira (may Allāh be well pleased with him) is reported as having said: "Allāh's Messenger (Allāh bless him and give him peace) once said:

> 'When the Day of Resurrection [*Yawm al-Qiyāma*] has finally arrived, and all creatures have been gathered together on a single piece of high ground "for a Day of which there is no doubt [*li-Yawmin lā raiba fīh*],"[13] a black shadow will envelop them, and the darkness will be so intense that they will not be able to see one another. The assembled creatures will all be standing on the balls of their feet [as they try to peer upwards], even though the distance between them and their Lord (Almighty and Glorious is He) will still be that of a journey that normally takes seventy years to complete.'

---

13 An allusion to the words of Allāh (Almighty and Glorious is He): *Rabba-nā inna-ka Jāmiʿu 'n-nāsi li-yawmin lā raiba fī-h: inna 'llāha lā yukhlifu 'l-mīʿād.* **Our Lord, You are the One who shall gather mankind together for a Day of which there is no doubt. Allāh does not fail to keep the tryst. (3:9)**
fa-kaifa idhā jamaʿnā-hum li-yawmin lā raiba fī-h: wa wuffiyat kullu nafsin mā kasabat wa hum lā yuẓlamūn. **How [will it be with them] when We have brought them all together for a Day of which there is no doubt, when every soul shall be paid in full for what it has earned, and they shall not be wronged? (3:25)**

"He then went on to say (Allāh bless him and give him peace):

> 'While they are in that situation, the Creator [*al-Khāliq*] (Blessed and Exalted is He) will suddenly make Himself manifest to the angels. The earth will at once become radiant with the light of its Lord, and the darkness will vanish away. All those creatures will thus be enveloped by the light of their Lord, while the angels are circling around the Heavenly Throne [*ʿArsh*], hymning the praise of their Lord and celebrating His holiness.'

"He then continued (Allāh bless him and give him peace):

> 'While those creatures are all standing there in rows, with each religious community [*umma*] lined up in a separate area, the record sheets [*ṣuḥuf*] and the balance [*mīzān*] will suddenly be brought to the fore. The record sheets will be laid in the scale, while the balance is held suspended by the hand of one of the angels, and they will sometimes cause it to rise up high, and at other times to sink down low.'

"To this he added (Allāh bless him and give him peace):

> 'While they are in that state, lo and behold, the screen will suddenly be removed from the Garden of Paradise, which will then be brought nearer. A wind will blow forth from inside it, and the Muslims will discover that it has a fragrant aroma like musk, even though the distance between them and the Garden of Paradise is still that of a journey that normally takes five hundred years to complete.
>
> 'The lid will then be removed from Hell [*Jahannam*], and a wind will blow forth from it, together with a terrible cloud of smoke. The wicked sinners will thus discover that it has a stinking aroma, even though the distance between them and Hell is still that of a journey that normally takes five hundred years to complete.

'Hell will then be brought closer, dragged along by means of an enormous chain, to which it has been firmly tied. Nineteen keepers, chosen from among the angels, will be tugging at that chain, and each of those keepers will be accompanied by seventy thousand other angels, serving as his assistants. While each of the nineteen keepers, together with his assistants, takes a turn at dragging Hell along, the other keepers, together with their assistants, will be walking to the right and left of it, and following up behind it. Each and every angel amongst them will hold in his hand a grappling hook made of iron. They will shout and bellow as they goad Hell along, but its slow progress will be made to the accompaniment of moaning and sighing, staggering and stumbling, clouds of gloom and smoke, rattling and clanking noises, and a towering inferno stoked by the fury of its rage against its own inhabitants. Thus they will eventually install it in a position midway between the Garden of Paradise and the place where the resurrected creatures are kept standing [*al-mawqif*].

'At this point, Hell will lift its gaze. As soon as it spies the creatures assembled there, it will bolt towards them in order to devour them. Its keepers will have to pull on its chains to hold it in check, for if it were left to its own devices, it would pounce upon every believer [*mu'min*] and unbeliever [*kāfir*] without distinction. Once it sees that it has been effectively restrained from attacking the assembled throng of creatures, it will simmer and boil with an intensity that can hardly be distinguished from the most furious kind of rage. Then it will heave another sigh, and the resurrected creatures will hear the sound of the gnashing of its teeth. This will cause their hearts to shudder and tremble with alarm. They will fly into a state of panic, their eyes will glaze over, and their hearts will end up in their throats.'"

According to another report, somebody once said: "O Prophet of Allāh, describe Hell to us!" He responded to this (Allāh bless him and give him peace) by saying:

> Very well. Like this earth in magnitude. Seventy degrees of longitude. Dark black. It has seven heads, and each of its heads has thirty doors. The length of each of its doors is equal to the distance of a journey that would take three nights. Its upper lip protrudes against its nose, while it trails its lower lip on the ground. In each of its nostrils there is a shackle and enormous chain, which is held in the grasp of seventy thousand angels, all of them rough, stern, their teeth grimly gritted, their eyes like live coals, and their colours like the flames of fire. While their nostrils give vent to lofty columns of flame and smoke, they stand at the ready, prepared at all times to receive and carry out the command of the All-Compelling One [*al-Jabbār*] (Blessed and Exalted is He).

Then the Prophet (Allāh bless him and give him peace) went on to say:

> There will come a moment when Hell [*Jahannam*] asks its Lord (Almighty and Glorious is He) for permission to perform an act of worshipful prostration [*sujūd*]. He will give it permission to do so, and Hell will thereupon adopt an attitude of prostration for as long as Allāh wills. Then the All-Compelling One [*al-Jabbār*] (Almighty and Glorious is He) will say: "Now raise your head!"

He continued (Allāh bless him and give him peace):

> Hell will raise its head at once, saying: "Praise be to Allāh, who has made me the instrument by which He exacts retribution from those who disobey Him, and has not made anything in the whole of His creation an instrument by which to exact retribution from me!"

To this he added (Allāh bless him and give him peace):

> Then Hell will say, over and over again, with a tongue that is fluent [*ṭaliq*] and eloquent [*dhaliq*] and smooth [*saliq*]: "Praise be to Allāh [*al-ḥamdu li'llāh*]!" For as long as Allāh wills, it will go on repeating this declaration of praise, in a loud voice peculiar to itself alone.
>
> Then Hell will heave a deep sigh, which will so affect those who hear it that not a single one of them will fail to sink down on his knees – not one angel brought near to the Lord [*mal'ak muqarrab*], not one Prophet sent as a Messenger [*Nabī Mursal*], and not one of those resurrected creatures who are present at the place of standing [*al-mawqif*].
>
> Then Hell will heave a second deep sigh, and not a single eye that still has a drop of moisture in it will fail to shed a tear.
>
> Then Hell will heave a third deep sigh, and even if those who hear that sigh – be they human beings or jinn – were each endowed with the merit of seventy-two Prophets, they would surely be moved to embrace her as a man embraces a woman [*la-wāqaʿū-hā*].[14]
>
> Then Hell will heave a fourth deep sigh, and nothing that is capable of speech will fail to have its speech arrested. The only exceptions will be Gabriel, Michael, and [Abraham] the Bosom Friend [*Khalīl*] of the All-Merciful One [*ar-Raḥmān*] (Almighty and Glorious is He), each one of whom will say, as they cling to the Heavenly Throne [*ʿArsh*]: "My own soul, my own soul [*nafsī, nafsī*] – that is all I beg You to spare!"

---

14 In Arabic, the words *Jahannam* [Hell], *an-Nār* [the Fire of Hell], *al-Janna* [the Garden of Paradise], *ad-dunyā* [this world] and *al-ākhira* [the hereafter] are grammatically feminine. This makes it easy for an Arabic speaker or writer to personify them as female beings, if he wishes to represent them as characters in a parable, rather than as abstract entities.

The Prophet (Allāh bless him and give him peace) continued:

> Then Hell will send forth a shower of sparks, as numerous as the stars. Each spark will be like an enormous cloud arising in the West, and that shower of sparks will fall upon the heads of the assembled creatures.

He went on to say (Allāh bless him and give him peace):

> Then the Bridge [*Ṣirāṭ*] will be erected over Hell. Seven hundred arches will be made ready to support it, and the distance between each pair of arches will be that of a journey taking seventy years.[15] The dimensions of the Bridge [*Ṣirāṭ*] will be as follows: from the first platform down to the second platform, the distance of a journey taking five hundred years; from the second down to the third, the distance of a journey taking five hundred years; from the third down to the fourth, the same distance again; from the fourth down to the fifth, the same distance again; from the fifth down to the sixth, the same distance again; and from the sixth down to the seventh, likewise. This seventh platform will be the widest of them all, the hottest of them all, the most deeply concave of them all, the most varied of them all [in its range of torments], and the most fiery of them all - by a factor of seventy.
>
> As for the lowest platform, its flames will rise up past the Bridge on the right side and the left, as they soar into the sky to a distance of three miles. Each platform will be hotter, more thickly littered with live coals, and beset with more varied kinds of torment than the one above it - by a factor of seventy.
>
> Upon each platform there will be an ocean, rivers, mountains and trees. The height of each of those mountains, as it towers up into the

15 Author's note: According to one version of this report, there will be seven arches [rather than seven hundred].

sky, will be equal to the distance of a journey taking seventy thousand years. There will be seventy such mountains on each platform, and on each mountain there will be seventy thousand separate hills. On each of those separate hills there will be seventy thousand thorny trees [*shajara ḍarīʿ*].[16] Each of those trees will have seventy branches, and there will be seventy serpents and seventy scorpions lurking on each of its branches. Each of those serpents will be three miles in length, and as for the scorpions, they will resemble huge Bactrian camels. Seventy thousand pieces of fruit will be dangling from each of those trees, and each piece of fruit will have the shape of a devil's head. Inside almost every one of those pieces of fruit there will be seventy worms, and each of those worms will be exceedingly long. Some pieces of fruit will not contain worms, but they will have thorns inside them instead.

The Prophet (Allāh bless him and give him peace) also used to say:

Hell [*Jahannam*] has seven entrances, and each of those entrances has seventy valleys. The depth of each of those valleys is the distance of a journey taking seventy years. Each of those valleys has seventy thousand branches, and in each of its branches there are seventy thousand caves. In each of those caves there are seventy thousand crevices, and each of its crevices extends to the distance of a journey taking seventy years. Seventy thousand snakes are lurking inside each of those crevices, and there are seventy thousand scorpions inside the jaws of each of those snakes. Each of those scorpions has

---

16 Like *zaqqūm*, the infernal food called *ḍarīʿ* is mentioned in the Qurʾān, in the words of Allāh (Almighty and Glorious is He): *laisa la-hum ṭaʿāmun illā min ḍarīʿ*. **There shall be no food for them except *aḍ-ḍarīʿ*. (88:6)** According to the Arabic lexicographers, *aḍ-ḍarīʿ* is a "certain plant in water that has become altered for the worse by long standing or the like, having roots that do not reach the ground," or "a certain thing in Hell, more bitter than aloes, and more stinking than the carcass, and hotter than the fire." See: E.W. Lane, *Arabic-English Lexicon*, art. *D-R-ʿ*. (Pickthall translates *aḍ-ḍarīʿ* as "bitter thorn-fruit.")

> seventy thousand spinal columns, and each of its spinal columns contains a flask of poison. Neither the unbeliever [*kāfir*] nor the hypocrite [*munāfiq*] will reach his final destination without experiencing all this to the full.

He also said (Allāh bless him and give him peace):

> While the assembled creatures are down on their knees, and Hell is prancing about like a camel in heat, a herald will issue a proclamation in a very loud voice. The Prophets [*anbiyā'*], the champions of truth [*ṣiddīqūn*], the martyrs [*shuhadā'*] and the righteous [*ṣāliḥūn*] will thereupon spring to their feet. Then they will offer a proposal, to the effect that wrongs should be set right. Then they will offer a second proposal, the effect of which will be that the disembodied spirits [*arwāḥ*] and the physical bodies [*ajsād*] engage in mutual debate, and that the physical bodies win the argument against the disembodied spirits. Then they will offer a third proposal to Allāh (Almighty and Glorious is He), as a result of which the record sheets [*ṣuḥuf*] will fly up into the air – and fall into the hands of the people assembled at the place of Resurrection. One person will have his record given to him in his right hand, another will have his record given to him in his left hand, and yet another will have his record given to him behind his back.
>
> As for those who receive their records with their right hands, they will be granted a light from the Light of their Lord, and the angels will congratulate them on their mark of honour. They will then pass over the Bridge [*Ṣirāṭ*], through the mercy of their Lord, and proceed to enter their Gardens of Paradise. Their guardians will be waiting to meet them at the gates of their Gardens of Paradise, ready to present them with their garments and their riding mounts, and to equip them with all the finery that will suit them best.

They will then disperse to their respective dwellings, and gleefully make tracks towards their palatial mansions, where they will enter into the company of their spouses. They will see sights that their tongues could never have described, that their eyes have never beheld, and the very idea of which has never occurred to their hearts. They will eat and drink, and put on their fine new clothes and ornaments. They will then embrace their spouses, to the utmost extent of which they are capable.

Then they will offer praise to their Creator [*Khāliq*], who has banished their sorrow from them, replaced their sense of anxiety with a feeling of security, and made their reckoning an easy matter for them to undergo. Then they will express their gratitude for all that their Lord has bestowed upon them. They will say: "Praise be to Allāh [*al-ḥamdu li'llāh*], who has guided us to this, for we could not have guided ourselves, if Allāh had not guided us." They will be highly delighted when they recognise the provisions they have obtained from their life in the lower world, for they were people of conviction [*mūqinīn*], people of faith [*mu'minīn*], believers in the truth [*muṣaddiqīn*], people whose fears and hopes and longings were focused on their Lord. That is the criterion by which the saved obtain salvation [*naja 'n-nājūn*], and by which the unbelievers are doomed to perdition [*halaka 'l-kāfirūn*].

As for those who receive their records with their left hands or from behind their backs, their faces will be darkly stained, the fair colour of their eyes will be altered, a brand will be stamped on the tips of their noses, their bodies will be bloated, and their skins will turn coarse and rough. They will cry out in woeful distress, when they look at their records and see their sins with their own eyes. Whatever the nature of the sins they committed in the past, be they minor or major offences, they will find them every single one of them substantiated in their records.

They will therefore be dejected in their feelings, and their thoughts will be filled with foreboding. Their alarm will be intense, and great will be their anxiety. Their heads will be bowed, their eyes downcast, and their necks bent low. They may try to steal a glance at the Fire of Hell that awaits them, but once they have looked, it will be impossible for them to withdraw their gaze from the sight, because they have laid their eyes upon something that is enormous, huge, horrifying, momentous, overwhelming, distressing, terrible, dreadful, tragic, repulsive, disturbing to the feelings and tear-provoking to the eyes.

They will thus acknowledge their servitude to their Lord. They will confess their sins, and they will experience their confession as a scorching fire, a shameful disgrace, a sorrowful affliction, a painful agony, a compulsory obligation, and an extremely distasteful necessity.

He then went on to say (Allāh bless him and give him peace):

While the people are down on their knees, confessing their sins in the presence of their Lord (Almighty and Glorious is He), their eyes will be so obscured that they cannot see clearly, their feelings will be so downcast that they cannot think rationally, and their limbs will be trembling so violently that they cannot produce articulate speech. Their bonds of kinship will be severed, so that they cannot connect with one another. There will therefore be no family ties to link them together on that day, and they will not be responsible for one another. They will be stricken with such personal loss that they cannot recuperate. They may beg for a second chance, but their pleading will go unanswered. They will have to acknowledge

> the truth of that which they used to dismiss as false, for now they are thirsty and unable to quench their thirst, hungry and unable to satisfy their hunger, naked and unable to clothe their nakedness, defeated and unable to triumph. They are stricken with grief and deprivation, having lost themselves and their families, their goods and their profits.

He also said (Allāh bless him and give him peace):

> While the people are in this condition, Allāh (Exalted is He) will suddenly command the keepers of Hell [*Jahannam*] to make their exit from it, together with their assistants, and to bring with them all their tools and instruments, such as chains, shackles and grappling hooks. They will thereupon emerge from Hell and take up a position outside it, while they wait to see what further orders they will be given.

He continued (Allāh bless him and give him peace):

> When the wretched people notice that the keepers have come out from Hell, and when they set eyes upon their fetters and their gear, they will start biting their own hands. They will eat their fingernails, then cry out in distress as their blood comes gushing forth. Their feet will shake and stumble, and they will despair of anything good. Then Allāh (Exalted is He) will give the order: "Seize them and tie them up, then roast them on the blazing Fire [*Jaḥīm*], then bind them securely in chains!"

He went on to say (Allāh bless him and give him peace):

> Whenever Allāh wishes to cast a group of people into those layers [of Hell], He summons their keepers and says to them: "Seize these people!" Seventy angels immediately rush towards each individual member of the group concerned. They tighten their bonds, putting

> heavy shackles on their necks and fixing chains through their noses. This causes them to be throttled, and their spinal columns are also broken to pieces, since their forelocks are bent over behind their backs and tied to their feet.

He also said (Allāh bless him and give him peace):

> Once they have been subjected to this treatment, their eyes will become glazed, their jugular veins will be inflated, the flesh of their necks will be scorched, and their blood vessels will be stripped bare. The heat of the shackles will burn into their heads, causing their brains to boil. Their brains will then spill out onto their outer layers of skin and trickle down to their feet. This will cause their outer layers of skin to peel off, and the fleshy parts beneath to turn green, as the pus flows out of them.
>
> When the shackles are placed on their necks, they will fill the whole area between their shoulders and their ears. Their fleshy parts will therefore be scorched, their lips will be hacked to pieces, their teeth will be exposed like fangs, and their tongues will stick out as they utter noises and screams. Those shackles will gleam with the glow of soaring flames, the heat of which will flow through their veins like blood, leaving them hollow. Since the flames of the Fire of Hell will also be flowing through them, the heat of those shackles will reach their hearts. Detached from their strings, their hearts will move up till they reach their throats, and this will intensify their strangulation. Their voices will be cut off completely, and their outer layers of skin will totally disappear.
>
> Then, while they are in this condition, Allāh (Exalted is He) will command the keepers of Hell [*Jahannam*] to provide them with clothing. They will dress them at once in shirts and trousers. These

garments will be extremely dark black in colour, reeking with the stench of decay, rough and coarse to the touch, and ablaze from the intensity of their heat. If they were set down on the mountains of the earth, they would cause them to melt away.

He continued (Allāh bless him and give him peace):

Then Allāh (Almighty and Glorious is He) will say to the keepers of Hell [*Jahannam*]: "Herd them away to their dwelling places!" They will thereupon produce another set of chains, longer and coarser than those in which the people had already been firmly secured. Each of the angels will then take one of those chains and use it to bind all the members of one of the religious communities [*umma mina 'l-umam*] together. Then he will place the end of the chain over his shoulder and turn his back on them. Then he will set off with them, dragging them along with their faces on the ground.

In the rear of each religious community there will be a team of seventy thousand angels, prodding its members with goading irons until they drive them to Hell, at the brink of which they will bring them to a halt.

He went on to say (Allāh bless him and give him peace):

At this point the angels will say to them: "This is the Fire of Hell, the reality of which you were in the habit of denying. Is this mere sorcery, or can you not see? Now you must roast in it, so you may or may not have the patience to endure, but that will not make the slightest difference as far as you are concerned. You are simply being repaid for what you used to do."

He also said (Allāh bless him and give him peace):

As soon as they have been brought to a halt at the brink of Hell, its

> gates will be opened to admit them and its covering will be removed to expose its contents. Its Fire will blaze and burst forth in flames, and a terrible cloud of smoke will then emerge from it, together with a hail of sparks, as numerous as the stars in the sky. These sparks will fly up high into the sky, to the distance of a journey taking seventy years. Then all of this will come back down, to fall on the heads of the people in chains. The hair on their heads will thus be consumed by fire, and their skulls will be cracked and shattered.

He continued (Allāh bless him and give him peace):

> Then Hell will scream in the loudest voice it can muster: "Come here to me, O people of the Fire, come here to me! By the Might and Glory of my Lord, I shall most certainly inflict retribution upon you!" Then it will say: "Praise be to Allāh, who has made me angry on account of His anger, and who is using me to inflict retribution upon His enemies. My Lord, add heat to my heat, and add strength to my strength!"

He went on to say (Allāh bless him and give him peace):

> Yet another set of angels will then come forth from Hell, and each one among them will approach one of the religious communities [*umma mina 'l-umam*]. He will pick up the members of that community at his leisure, and then topple them facedown into Hell. This means that they will land on their heads – eventually, since they will go on falling for the distance of a journey taking seventy years, before they reach the peaks of the mountains of Hell.

To this he added (Allāh bless him and give him peace):

> Even when they finally reach the peaks of the mountains of Hell, they will not alight upon those peaks until each and every individual amongst them has had his skin stripped and replaced no less than seventy times.

He also said (Allāh bless him and give him peace):

> The first meal they get to eat on those mountain peaks will be a meal consisting of the fruit called *az-zaqqūm*,[17] the heat of which is outwardly apparent, the bitterness of which is extremely intense, and the thorns of which are very many. While they are chewing that meal of theirs, the angels will suddenly come upon them, beating them with their goading irons till their bones are smashed to pieces. Then the angels will grab hold of them by their legs and fling them into Hell, so that they plunge headfirst for the distance of a journey taking seventy years, before landing on the outlying ridges of the mountains of Hell.

To this he added (Allāh bless him and give him peace):

> They will not alight upon those outlying ridges, however, until each and every individual amongst them has had his skin stripped and replaced no less than seventy times.

He also said (Allāh bless him and give him peace):

> That meal of theirs will be stuck in their mouths, for they will find it impossible to swallow and stomach. The food will thus combine with the heart to form a lump in the area of the gullet, causing a choking sensation. Each and every individual amongst them will then appeal for help in the form of something to drink. It will suddenly become apparent to them that, within those mountain ridges, there are river valleys streaming into Hell, so they will set off walking until they reach them, at which point they will bend down over them and attempt to drink the liquid they contain.

17 Allāh (Almighty and Glorious is He) first mentioned *zaqqūm* when He said: *inna shajarata 'z-zaqqūmi ṭaʿāmu 'l-athīm.* **The tree of *az-zaqqūm* is the food of the sinner. (44:43-44)** According to some Qur'ānic commentators, when the notorious Abū Jahl heard this revelation, he responded by saying: "Dates and fresh butter! We shall swallow it at our leisure." Allāh (Exalted is He) thereupon sent down a grim warning: **We have assigned it as a torment for the evildoers. It is a tree that sprouts at the very bottom of Hell. The spathes thereof are like heads of devils, and they must eat of it, and with it they must fill their bellies. (37:63-6)**

He continued (Allāh bless him and give him peace):

> The result of this will be that the skin is stripped from their faces, to be carried away in the current. They will find that it is actually impossible to drink from those streams, and so they will turn around and try to move away from them. The angels will be catching up with them, however, while they are still bending over those springs, and they will flog them till their bones are smashed to pieces. Then they will grab hold of them by their legs and fling them into Hell, so that they plunge headfirst for the distance of a journey taking one hundred and forty years, through blazing flames and a terrible cloud of smoke, before landing in those river valleys.

To this he added (Allāh bless him and give him peace):

> They will not alight upon those river valleys, however, until each and every individual amongst them has had his skin stripped and replaced no less than seventy times.

He went on to say (Allāh bless him and give him peace):

> The ultimate destination of the liquid that flows from those mountain springs is down in those river valleys. They will try to drink from it, but only to find that it is the fluid of Hell's inferno [*mā' al-Jaḥīm*]. It will not settle in their stomachs until Allāh has stripped and replaced the skin of each and every individual amongst them no less than seventy times.

To this he added (Allāh bless him and give him peace):

> As soon as some of that liquid has settled in their bellies, their intestines will be cut to pieces, which will then come out through their buttocks. The rest of it will flow through their veins, causing their fleshy parts to melt and their bones to crack. The angels will soon catch up with them, to beat them with their goading irons on

their faces, their backsides and their heads. Each goading iron of theirs has three hundred and sixty cutting edges, so when they are used to strike people on their heads, their skulls are smashed in and their spinal columns are shattered to bits. Then they are dragged into the Fire of Hell, lying flat upon their faces, until they find themselves right in the middle of its blazing inferno. The Fire will then consume their outer layers of skin, and burn its way into their ears. Its flames will thus emerge through their nostrils and their ribs, while the pus oozes out of their bodies. Their eyes will pop out of their sockets, to dangle down over their cheeks.

After all this, they will be joined together with those devils [*shayāṭīn*] of theirs, the ones they used to obey, and with those deities [*āliha*] of theirs, to whom they used to appeal for help. They will be thrown into places that are narrow and cramped, so they will cry out in their woe and distress, until their possessions are produced – only to be heated in their own fire, then used to brand them on their foreheads and their sides, then pressed down on their backs so that they come out through their bellies.

They have earned this treatment, for they are the friends of Hell [*awliyā᾽ Jahannam*] and the associates of the devils and the stones [*quranā᾽ ash-shayāṭīn wa 'l-ḥijāra*]. They piled up their sins like mountains, in order to make sure that their punishment would be very severe indeed. The height of one such mountain of sins is equal to the distance of a month-long journey, while its width is that of a five-day march, its thickness is that of a five-night trek, and its peak is like that of al-Aqraʿ, which is a mountain in the remotest part of Syria. In the face of that mountain there are thirty-two sharp teeth, some of which stick out from its head, while some of them appear beneath the bottom of its beard. Its nose is like an enormous hill. As

> for the length and coarseness of the hair on its head, it resembles the cedar tree, and the sheer abundance of it is like all the thickets of this world. Its upper lip is contracting, while the lower one is ninety cubits [*dhirā*ʿ] in length.[18] The length of its hand is equal to the distance of a ten-day journey, and the thickness of it is equal to that of a single day's march. Its thighs are like a couple of metal plates, and the thickness of its skin is forty cubits on its arm. The length of its leg is equivalent to the distance of a five-night journey, while the thickness of it is equal to that of a single day's march. Each pupil of its eyes resembles Ḥirāʾ, which is a mountain near Makkah. When tar is poured over its head, the fire inside it glows more brightly, for it can only add to its inflammation.

According to one traditional report, the Prophet (Allāh bless him and give him peace) used to say:

> By the One who holds my soul in His hand, if a man were to emerge from the Fire of Hell – dragging a chain, with his hands shackled to his neck, with shackles on his neck and iron fetters on his legs – and if his fellow creatures were then to catch sight of him, they would certainly flee from him and run as far away from him as they possibly could.

The traditional report continues:

> Due to the intensity of the heat of the Fire of Hell, its grievous affliction, the varied range of its torment, and the narrowness of its dwelling places, the fleshy parts of its inhabitants will turn green, their bones will split and crack, their brains will boil and pour down over their outer layers of skin. As their skin is burned away, their limbs will be cut off at the joints. Then, as the pus oozes out from

18 As a unit of length, the Arabic term *dhirā*ʿ – like the medieval English cubit – is based on the length of the forearm from the elbow to the tip of the middle finger. While it is usually equal to about 18 inches, it sometimes signifies a length of 21 inches or even more.

their dismembered limbs, their bodies will come to be riddled with maggots and worms. Those maggots and worms will soon grow so fat that they come to resemble the wild ass. They will also develop claws, and those claws of theirs will be just like the talons of vultures and eagles. They will burrow into the areas between the outer skin and the flesh of their victims, and rip them to shreds. They will give out a moaning sound in the process, and they will scurry to and fro, just as a frightened wild animal scurries to and fro. They will eat their victims' flesh and drink their blood, for they have no other form of food and drink.

The angels will come and seize those people, then drag them along with their faces down on the live coals and stones, which stick out from the ground as if they were teeth. They will keep dragging them along until they reach the ocean of Hell [*Jahannam*]. This means covering the distance of a journey taking seventy years, so they will not reach it until all their joints are broken, nor without having their skins stripped and replaced no fewer than seventy thousand times each day. When the angels finally bring them to their destination, they will hand them over to the keepers of the ocean of Hell, who will immediately grab them by their legs and shove them into it. No one knows the depth of that ocean, except the One who created it.

According to some accounts, the following description is recorded in one of the books of the Torah [*asfār at-Tawrāh*]:

The ocean of this world, by comparison with the ocean of Hell, is like a small well on the shore of the ocean of this world. So, when they are thrown into it, and experience the first touch of the torment it has to offer, they will say to one another: "As it seems now, the torment inflicted upon us before this was actually a form of gentle clemency."

The traditional report continues:

> They will sink down once, before rising again to the surface. Then the ocean will boil, as it plunges them down to a depth of seventy fathoms. The distance of each fathom will be equivalent to the distance of the East from the West. Then the angels will herd them together with their goading irons, beating them with these sharp rods and driving them back down to the very bottom of the ocean, to the distance of a journey taking seventy years. Their only food and drink will be what the ocean provides, so they will rise back up from its lowest depth, covering the distance of a journey taking one hundred and forty years.
>
> On reaching the surface, one of them will wish to pause for breath, so the angels will approach him with their goading irons, rushing towards him in order to give him a beating. This time, however, he will remember that, if he raises his head, seventy thousand goading irons will be aimed at that head of his. Since none of them ever misses its target, they will send him back down to a depth of seventy fathoms, each fathom being equivalent to the distance of the East from the West.

The traditional report continues further:

> They will stay in the ocean of Hell for as long as Allāh wills that this state of affairs should last. In the meantime, their flesh and bones will be eaten away, so that only their spirits survive. They will eventually be struck by a wave that rolls them along for seventy years, then casts them ashore on one of the beaches of the ocean of Hell. On that beach there are seventy thousand caves, and deep inside each cave there are seventy thousand crevices. Each of those crevices extends as far as a journey lasting seventy years, and lurking deep inside each crevice there are seventy thousand snakes. The length of

> each of those snakes is seventy cubits, and each of those snakes has seventy sharp fangs. Within each of those fangs there is a flask of poison, and lurking inside the jaws of each of those snakes there are a thousand scorpions. Each of those scorpions has seventy vertebrae, and in each of those vertebrae there is a flask of poison.

The traditional report goes on to tell us:

> Once their spirits have finally come ashore from that ocean of Hell, and have found their way into those caves, they will be provided with new bodies and new skins. Then they will be shackled in iron, at which point those serpents and scorpions will come out and attack them. Each and every individual amongst them will find that he has seventy thousand snakes and seventy thousand scorpions clinging to him. They will have no choice but to endure this onslaught with patience. Then the snakes and scorpions will climb up to their knees, and they will again have no choice but to endure the onslaught with patience. Then the snakes and scorpions will climb up to their chests, so they will yet again endure with patience. Then the snakes and scorpions will climb up to their collarbones, and patient endurance will once again be their only response. Then the snakes and scorpions will climb up higher still, attaching themselves to their noses, their lips, their teeth and their ears. At this point they will begin to panic, but they have nowhere to turn for refuge, except by running away into Hell, so into Hell they will tumble. As for the serpents, meanwhile, they will be chewing their flesh and sucking their blood, and as for the scorpions, they will be stinging them so hard that their fleshy parts will drop off piece by piece, and their limbs will be cut off at the joints. Even when they have tumbled into the Fire of Hell, it will take seventy years for the Fire to burn them clear of the poison injected into their systems by all those serpents and scorpions.

The traditional report continues:

> Then the Fire of Hell will burn them for seventy years, at the end of which time they will be equipped with new skins, different from the skins they had before. Then they will beg to be supplied with food, so the angels will bring them a special meal, ironically called "the wedding feast [*al-walīma*]" which is actually as dry and as hard as iron. They will attempt to chew it, but they will find it quite impossible to eat the slightest morsel of it, so they will spit it out of their mouths. They will then set about devouring their own hands, as the only way to satisfy the extreme intensity of their hunger. They will begin by eating their fingertips and their palms. Once they have eaten those, they will start on their forearms and eat them too, as far as their elbows. Then they will start on their elbows, and go on eating all the way up to their shoulders, until only the tips of their shoulders are left uneaten. If they could get their mouths to reach any part of their bodies after that, they would certainly eat that part as well! After they have done all this to their bodies, however, they will be suspended from the tree called *az-zaqqūm* by means of iron flesh-hooks attached to their Achilles' tendons [*ʿarāqīb*].

The traditional report continues further:

> Seventy thousand of them will be suspended from a single branch, with their heads hanging downward, yet this will not cause the branch to bend. Then the blazing inferno will be ignited beneath them, and the heat of the Fire of Hell will rise to scorch their faces. This will go on for a period of seventy years, so that their bodies will melt away and only their spirits will survive intact.
>
> Then they will be supplied with fresh skins and new bodies. But then they will be suspended once again, this time by their fingertips, with the flames of the Fire of Hell beneath them. Those flames will rise

and penetrate inside them through their buttocks, consuming their hearts before eventually emerging from their noses, their mouths and their ears. This process will also go on for a period of seventy years, so that their bones and their flesh will melt away and only their spirits will survive intact.

Then they will be granted a brief respite, while they are supplied with fresh skins and new bodies. But then they will be suspended once again, this time by their eyes, for the same length of time and with similar consequences.

They will not cease to be tormented in this fashion, until there is not one joint in their bodies by which they have yet to be suspended, and not a single hair on their heads by which they have yet to be left dangling. Even though death approaches them from every joint in their bodies, they will not turn into lifeless corpses, while yet another ghastly torment is lying in wait behind them. Finally, when this particular form of punishment has been inflicted on them in every detail, the angels will bring them down from the branch of the tree. They will then take each and every individual amongst them off to his dwelling place, shackled with a chain and dragged along with his face to the ground.

The traditional report goes on to tell us:

The dimensions of their dwelling places in Hell will be commensurate with their wicked deeds. One of them, for instance, will be assigned to a lodging the length of which is equal to a month-long journey, and the width of which is similar. A fire will be ignited in it, and no one else will share it with him. Another of them, meanwhile, will be assigned to a lodging of which both the length and width correspond to a journey of only twenty-nine nights. Yet others will

> be assigned to progressively smaller and narrower lodgings, till the point is reached where one of them is given a lodging that measures the equivalent of a one-day journey in both length and width.
>
> The torments inflicted on them will match the size of their lodgings, so they will be in several different postures while receiving their punishment. One of them will take his punishment while standing on his head. One of them will take his punishment in a sitting position. One of them will take his punishment while squatting down on his knees. One of them will take his punishment while standing on his legs. One of them will take his punishment while sprawled out flat on his belly. In each of these lodgings, the breathing space available to the occupants will be narrower than the tip of a spear.
>
> The height of the fire inside the various lodgings will also vary. In one case, the fire will reach up to the ankles of the occupant. One of them will be in fire up to his knees. One of them will be in fire up to his waist. One of them will be in fire up to his navel. One of them will be in fire up to his collar bone. One of them will be completely immersed in a flood of fire, which will sometimes lift him up to the surface, and sometimes spin him around, as it plunges him down into its depths to the distance of a month-long journey.
>
> Once they have settled into their dwelling places, they will all link up with their comrades, and weep until their tears run dry. Then they will shed tears of blood, to the point where ships could be launched in the current of their tears.

The traditional report continues:

> They will have one day to spend together in the pit of the blazing inferno, after which there will never be another opportunity for

> them to congregate. When Allāh (Almighty and Glorious is He) gives permission on that day, a herald will cry out in the pit of the blazing inferno, and his voice will be heard by those at the very top and those at the very bottom, by those who are nearest to the centre and those who are at the farthest edge. This is what is called the Gathering [*al-Ḥashr*]. The herald will say: "O people of the Fire of Hell, assemble together!" In response to this summons, they will all assemble together in the pit of the blazing inferno of Hell [*al-Jaḥīm*], accompanied by the tormenting angels [*zabāniya*].[19]

The traditional report goes on to tell us:

> The people of the Fire of Hell will then start arguing with one another. Those who used to be despised will say to those who were scornful: "We used to be your followers in the world below,[20]
>
> *fa-hal antum mughnūna ʿan-nā min ʿadhābi 'llāhi min shai.*
> **So will you be of any help to us at all in the face of Allāh's punishment?" (14:21)**

19 In the verse [*āya*] of the Qurʾān (96:18), Allāh (Exalted is He) declares: "**We shall summon the '*zabāniya*'.**" Since the trilateral Arabic root *Z-B-N* conveys the idea of "shoving" or "thrusting", the commentators have understood the term to mean "certain angels, so called because they are charged with the task of thrusting the damned into the Fire of Hell." In the Fifth Discourse of The Removal of Cares [*Jala al-Khawāṭir*] Shaikh ʿAbd al-Qādir al-Jīlānī (may Allāh be well pleased with him) tells us that the Prophet (Allāh bless him and give him peace) is reported as having said:
Allāh (Almighty and Glorious is He) has created tormenting angels [*zabāniya*] within the Fire of Hell. They serve Allāh by inflicting vengeance on His enemies, the unbelievers. So, when He wishes to chastise an unbeliever [*kāfir*], He says to them: "Seize him!" Seventy thousand of them immediately rush towards the unbeliever, and as soon as he falls into the hands of one of them, he melts like fat in the fire, so that nothing is left on his body but the dripping [*wadak*]. Then Allāh (Almighty and Glorious is He) restores his normal constitution to him, whereupon they proceed to bind him with shackles and chains of fire, tying his head and his feet together. Then they hurl him unto the Fire of Hell.

20 A slightly paraphrased version of the Qurʾānic verse [*āya*]: *fa-qāla 'ḍ-ḍuʿafāʾu li 'lladhīna 'stakbarū innā kunnā lakum tabaʿan.* **Then the weak will say to those who were proud: "We used to be your followers." (14:21)**

Those who were proud will say:
innā kullun fī-hā inna 'llāha qad ḥakama baina 'l-'ibād.
"Every one of us is in it; indeed, Allāh has already passed judgement on His servants." (40:48)

Those who were proud will also say to those who used to be despised: "You may turn to us for help, but for you there is no word of welcome here!" Those who used to be despised will then say to those who were proud:
al antum lā marḥaban bi-kum antum qaddamtumū-hu la-nā fa-bi'sa 'l-qarār.
"No, you are the ones for whom there is no word of welcome! You prepared this for us in advance, and how evil is the outcome!" (38:60)

Those who used to be despised will take exception to hearing this from those who were proud, and they will say:
Rabba-nā man qaddama la-nā hādhā fa-zid-hu 'adhāban ḍi'fan fi 'n-nār.
"Our Lord, whoever did prepare this for us, be sure to give him a double portion of torment in the Fire of Hell!" (38:61)

In response to this, those who were proud will say:
law hadā-na 'llāhu la-hadainā-kum.
"If Allāh had guided us aright, we would surely have guided you aright." (14:21)

Those who used to be despised will then say to those who were proud: "**Not so! [You were only interested in your] scheming by night and day, when you were instructing us to disbelieve**

> **in Allāh, and to set up rivals in competition with Him. (34:33)** This means that we are untainted by you, and that we are innocent of the things you invited us to do in the lower world."

The traditional report continues:

> Then all of them will turn towards the devils [*shayāṭīn*] who are their fellow inmates, and the latter will tell them: "We led you into error, as we tempted you and lured you away from the right path." Eventually, when they have finished saying what they have to say on this subject, Satan himself [*ash-Shaiṭān*] will proclaim, in a high-pitched voice peculiar to him:
>
> "**Allāh surely promised you a promise of truth (14:22),** and Allāh summoned you, but you did not respond to His call, and you did not believe that His promise was true.
>
> "**I made you a promise, too, but then I let you down, for I had no authority over you, except that I called to you and you obeyed me. So do not lay the blame on me, but blame yourselves. I cannot come to your aid, nor can you be of any assistance to me (14:22)**, for I am quite ungrateful, on this day, for the fact that you rendered worshipful service to me, instead of to Allāh."

The traditional report continues, citing the words of Allāh (Almighty and Glorious is He):

> *fa-adhdhana mu'adhdhinun baina-hum an la'natu 'llāhi 'alā 'ẓ-ẓālimīn.*
>
> **And then a herald in between them will cry out: "The curse of Allāh is on the evildoers!" (7:44)**

Then the traditional report goes on to tell us:

> At this point, those who used to be despised will curse those who were proud, and those who were proud will curse those who used

to be despised. All of them will curse the devils who are their fellow inmates, and their fellow inmates will curse them in return. Then they will say to those fellow inmates of theirs: "If only we were separated from you by the distance that separates the two horizons from each other – for you are evil companions[21] for us today, just as you were evil ministers [*wuzarā'*] for us in the lower world."

When it finally dawns on them that they are all lumped together in a single congregation, they will start saying to one another: "Come on! Let us go and look for the custodians of this place. Perhaps they will intercede on our behalf in the presence of their Lord, so that He may relieve us of the torment for a day."

The traditional report continues further:

In spite of this, however, they will continue to suffer torment. The keepers of Hell will stay out of their reach for as long as seventy years, and then, when they eventually come round to them, they will say:

a-wa-lam taku ta'tī-kum rusulu-kum bi-'l bayyināt.

"Did your Messengers not come to you with clear proofs?" (40:50)

"Yes indeed," they will all respond together, whereupon the keepers of Hell will say:

fa- 'd'ū: wa mā du'ā'u 'l-kāfirīna illā fī ḍalāl.

"Then make your plea, although the pleading of the unbelievers is in vain." (40:50)

21 Up to this point, the sentence beginning, "If only..." is almost identical – except that the pronouns and one noun are in the plural instead of the singular – with the Qur'ānic verses [*āya*] in which Allāh (Exalted is He) has told us: *ḥattā idhā jā'a-nā qāla yā laita bainī bainaka bu'du 'l-mashriqaini fa-bi'sa 'l-qarīn.* **Till, when he comes to Us, he says "If only I were separated from you by the distance that separates the two horizons from each other for you are an evil companion." (43:38)**

Then, according to the same traditional report:

> When they see that the keepers of Hell will not do them any good, they will turn to the angel Mālik[22] with their next appeal for help, as they cry:
> **"O Mālik, let your Lord make an end of us! (43:77)** Let Him finally put us to death!"
>
> Mālik will keep them waiting for as long as it would take to travel the world, withholding his answer and declining to give them any response. Then, when he finally condescends to address them, it will be to say:
> **"You will have to linger on (43:77)** for many aeons of time, before He finally puts you to death!"
>
> When they see that Mālik will not do them any good, they will address their appeal for help directly to their Lord. To Him they will say:
> *Rabba-nā akhrij-nā min-hā fa-in ʿudnā fa-innā ẓālimūn.*
> **"Our Lord, bring us forth out of it! Then, if we revert, we shall be evildoers indeed." (23:107)**
> – That is to say, "if we revert to our former habit of disobeying You."

Then, as the traditional report goes on to tell us:

> The All-Compelling One [*al-Jabbār*] (Glory be to Him and Exalted is He) will keep them waiting for as long as seventy years. During all that time, He will neither respond to their request nor provide them with any benefit. Then, when He finally does reply to them in His own words, He will reduce them to the status of dogs, for He will say:
> [*qāla*] *'khsaʾū fī-hā wa lā tukallimūn.*
> **"Slink away into it, and do not speak to Me." (23:108)**

---

22 The literal meaning of the Arabic word *mālik* is "someone in authority; an owner or possessor." Mālik is the name of the angel who presides over Hell, superintending the torments inflicted on its occupants.

The traditional report continues further:

> When they see that their Lord will not bestow His mercy on them, and that He will not grant them any favour, they will say to one another, referring to their torment:
>
> *sawāʾun ʿalai-nā a-jaziʿnā am ṣabarnā mā la-nā min maḥīṣ.*
>
> **"It is all the same for us whether we writhe in agony, or whether we patiently endure; we have no place of refuge." (14:21)**
>
> *fa-mā la-nā min shāfiʿīn wa lā ṣadīqin ḥamīm: fa-law anna la-nā karratan fa-nakūna mina ʾl-muʾminīn.*
>
> **"Now we have no intercessors, nor any loyal friend. If only we could have another turn [on earth], so that we might be numbered among the believers." (26:100-102)**

The traditional report recounts what will happen to them next:

> Then, as the angels are taking them away to their dwelling places, their feet will slip and stumble. Any argument they try to make will be refuted, and they will see what their Lord (Almighty and Glorious is He) has in store for them. They will lose all hope of His mercy, and their sense of despair will throw them into a state of terrible distress. A profound awareness of shame and degradation will descend upon them, so they will sadly bemoan the loss of all the opportunities they squandered in the course of their worldly lives.
>
> As well as having their own heavy burdens loaded on their necks, they will also have to carry the burdens of those who used to be their followers and attendants, without the slightest reduction in those burdens of theirs. Their torments will be more numerous than the specks of dust on the earth and the drops of water in the oceans. They will be accompanied by some of the guardians of Hell

> [*zabāniya*] whose orders are abrupt, whose manner of speaking is harsh and crude, whose bodies are as prodigious as the lightning in the sky, whose faces are like live coals, whose eyes are like flames, whose colouring is dark and gloomy, whose teeth and nails are like the horns of cattle. The goading irons they hold in their hands are long, heavy and fiercely hot; if they used them to strike the mountains, the mountains would be split asunder by the force of the blow, then crumble like rotten old bones. The guardians of Hell will use these instruments to beat the sinners who have disobeyed their Lord, so those sinners will have every reason to shed tears of blood, once their ordinary tears have run dry. They may plead with their tormentors, but their pleas will go unanswered. They may weep and sob for mercy, but the *zabāniya* will show them no compassion. They may beg for a drink of cold water, but the only liquid they get from the guardians of Hell will be a kind of pus that roasts their faces.

According to the same traditional report, the Prophet (Allāh bless him and give him peace) used to say:

> An enormous cloud will gather each day, then drift over the people of the Fire of Hell. The flashes of lightning from it will dazzle their eyes, its thunder will crash down on their backs, and it will cast a gloom so dense that they cannot even see their hellish guardians. Then the cloud will proclaim, in its own peculiar booming voice: "O people of the Fire of Hell, would you not like me to give you a shower of rain?" They will all respond in chorus: "Shower us with cold water!" But the cloud will subject them for an hour to a hail of stones, which will fall on their heads and smash their skulls to pieces. Then it will rain upon them for another hour, this time with streams of boiling water, live coals in great abundance, smokeless flames of fire, and sharp hooks of iron. Then, for the next hour, it will shower them with snakes, scorpions, maggots and worms, and filthy slime.

The traditional report continues:

> Whenever it rains in Hell [*Jahannam*], the ocean of Hell becomes full to overflowing, so its depths begin to surge in waves and it heaves in a mighty rage. It leaves neither shore nor mountain in Hell uncovered by its rising tide, and so it submerges all the people of the Fire, although they do not die.

The traditional report continues further:

> The torments of Hell [*Jahannam*] will thus become worse and worse for those disobedient sinners, as conditions there become more and more extreme in every respect. Since they have incurred the retribution of their Lord, those who are doomed to reside there must suffer increasing degrees of harshness, heat, wailing and moaning, fire and smoke, darkness and gloom, stress and strain, poisonous fumes, boiling water, blazing and scorching, and every kind of agony.

Let us therefore take refuge from it with Allāh (Almighty and Glorious is He) – and from the deeds that lead to it, as well as from the companionship of its people! O Allāh, our Lord and its Lord, do not cause us to arrive within its confines! Do not place its shackles upon our necks! Do not clothe us with its garments! Do not feed us with its bitter fruit called *az-zaqqūm* and do not make us drink its boiling liquid! Do not put its keepers in charge of us! Do not treat us as fuel for its fire! By Your mercy, enable us instead to cross safely over its Bridge [*Ṣirāṭ*], and deflect its sparks and flames away from us, in order that You may deliver us, through Your mercy, from it and from its smoke, and from its grief and its torment. Amin, O Lord of All the Worlds!

The Prophet (Allāh bless him and give him peace) also used to say:

> If even the least impressive door of Hell were to be opened in the West, it would cause the mountains of the East to evaporate, just as drops of rain evaporate in the heat of the sun. If even a single spark

> from Hell were to fly out and fall in the West, while a man was in the East, his brain would boil and spill out over his body.
> Among all the inhabitants of the Fire of Hell, those who suffer the mildest torment are men who are forced to wear shoes made of fire, which emerges through their ears and their noses, and which causes their brains to boil. Next come those who are hurled down onto one of the rocks of Hell, so that they bounce off it, just as a grain of corn bounces out of a hot frying pan, and each time they fall off one rock they land upon another.

This means that all the inhabitants of the Fire of Hell are made to suffer torments commensurate with the wickedness of their respective deeds. Let us therefore take refuge with Allāh from their deeds and their destination!

The Prophet (Allāh bless him and give him peace) has told us:

> As for the torment inflicted on those who do not protect their private parts, they will be suspended by their genital organs for as long as they lived in this world, so that their physical bodies will disintegrate completely and only their spirits will survive intact. Then they will be released, to be equipped with new bodies and fresh skins. Then they will be tormented all over again. Every individual amongst them will be flogged by seventy thousand angels, for a period corresponding to his lifetime in this world, so that their physical bodies will disintegrate completely and only their spirits will survive intact. Such will be their punishment.
>
> As for the torment inflicted on the thief, he will be dismembered limb by limb, then put together again. That will be the extent of his punishment, except that each individual among the class of thieves will also be assaulted by seventy thousand angels, armed with large razor blades.

> As for the torment inflicted on those who give false witness, they will be suspended by their tongues. Then each individual amongst them will be flogged by seventy thousand angels, so that their physical bodies will disintegrate completely and only their spirits will survive intact.
>
> As for the torment inflicted on those who attribute partners to Allāh [*al-mushrikīn*], they will be lodged in the cavern of Hell, which will then be sealed to keep them from escaping. Inside that cavern, they will find themselves in the midst of snakes, scorpions, many live coals, and fierce flames and smoke. Every hour, each individual amongst them will have his skin stripped and renewed no fewer than seventy thousand times.
>
> As for the torment inflicted on cruel and arrogant tyrants, they will be placed in coffins made of fire. Then locks will be fastened to keep them inside, and the coffins will be deposited in the lowest tier of the Fire of Hell. Every hour, each individual amongst them will be subjected to ninety-nine different kinds of torment. Each of them will have his skin stripped and renewed a thousand times every day. Such will be their punishment.

According to the traditional report, the Prophet (Allāh bless him and give him peace) went on to say:

> As for those who are guilty of the betrayal of trust, they will bring their trickery with them. Then they will be thrown into the ocean of Hell [*Jahannam*]. To ensure that they go down all the way to the very bottom of it – the depth of which is known to none but the One who created it – they will then be told: "You must dive down deep, in order to get rid of your fraudulent deceit!"

> On hearing this, they will dive as deep as Allāh wills. Then they will return to the surface, sticking their heads out as they gasp for breath. At this point, however, each one of them will be assailed immediately by seventy thousand angels, each of them armed with a goading prong made of iron, ready to be swung against his head. Such will be their punishment forever.

According to the same traditional report, the Prophet (Allāh bless him and give him peace) also used to say:

> Allāh has condemned the people of the Fire of Hell to remain in it for aeons [*aḥqāb*]. While I do not know how many those aeons will be, I can tell you that a single aeon [*ḥuqb*] is a period of eighty thousand years, and that a year is three hundred and sixty days. In the context of Hell, however, one day is the equivalent of a thousand years by your reckoning.

Woe, therefore, to the people of the Fire of Hell! Woe to those faces – those faces that used to regard the heat of the sun as more than they could bear – at the time when the Fire is scorching them! Woe to those heads – those heads that used to regard an ordinary headache as more than they could bear – at the time when Hell's boiling water [*ḥamīm*] is being poured on top of them! Woe to those eyes – those eyes that used to regard ophthalmia [*ramad*] as more than they could bear – at the time when they are losing their colour and glazing over within the Fire of Hell! Woe to those ears – those ears that used to take such delight in listening to gossip and scandal – at the time when the flames are flaring out of them! Woe to those noses – those noses that used to twitch in discomfort at the smell of decaying corpses – at the time when they are having to inhale the Fire of Hell! Woe to those necks – those necks that used to regard the slightest ache or pain as more than they could bear – at the time when shackles are being fastened to them! Woe to those skins – those skins that used to regard coarse clothing material as more than they could bear – at the time when they are being clad in garments made from a fiery material that is coarse indeed to the touch, that gives off a stinking odour, and that is smoldering with fire! Woe to those bellies – those bellies that used to regard an ordinary stomach-ache as more than they could bear – at the time when the bitter fruit called *az-zaqqūm* combined with boiling water, is entering inside them and cutting their intestines to pieces! Woe to those feet – those feet that used to regard the slightest soreness as more than they could bear – at the time when they are being forced to wear shoes made of fire!

Woe to the people of the Fire of Hell, in all their varied torments! O Allāh, by virtue of this stupendous knowledge, and of Your universal grace and favour, do not cause us to be numbered among its inhabitants!

On crossing the bridge of Hell and entering the Garden of Paradise, as explained by the Prophet (Allāh bless him and give him peace) in a traditional report that has been handed down to us on the authority of Abū Huraira (may Allāh be well pleased with him)

According to Abū Huraira (may Allāh be well pleased with him), Allāh's Messenger (Allāh bless him and give him peace) used to say:

> The bridge of Hell [*jisr Jahannam*] has seven arches. The distance between each pair of arches is equal to that of a journey taking seventy years, while the width of the bridge is like the sharp edge of a sword. The first group of people will cross over it as quickly as it takes to blink an eye. The second group, at the speed of a brief flash of lightning. The third group, at the speed of a violent gust of wind. The fourth group, at the speed of birds. The fifth group, at the speed of horses. The sixth group, at the speed of a man in a hurry. As for the seventh group, they will cross over it at an ordinary walking pace.

When all seven groups have crossed over, one man will still be waiting, which means that he will be the very last to cross that bridge. "Cross over!" he will be told, so he will set his two feet upon it, but one of them will slip. Then he will straddle the bridge and try crawling along it on his knees, but the Fire of Hell will lick at his hair and his skin as he does so.

He will continue to wriggle along on his belly, for his other foot will slip, leaving him with one hand holding fast, while the other hand dangles loose. The Fire of Hell will attack him in that position, so he will suppose that he has no chance of escaping from its clutches. Nevertheless, he will continue to wriggle along on his belly, until he finally succeeds in getting beyond its reach. As soon as he is clear of it, he will look at it and say: "Blessed be the One who has delivered me from you! I cannot imagine that my Lord has ever given anyone, in ancient or modern times, the likes of what He has given me! He did indeed deliver me from you, after I had seen you and met you face to face!"

One of the angels will then approach him, take him by the hand, and lead him to a pond in front of the entrance to the Garden of Paradise. The angel will say to him: "Bathe yourself in this pond, and drink from it."

He will thereupon bathe himself in the pond, and take a drink from it. As he does so, the sweet aroma of the people of the Garden of Paradise will keep wafting towards him, and he will catch glimpses of their many colours. Then the angel will lead him away and make him stand at the entrance to the Garden of Paradise, saying to him: "Stand here and wait, until you receive permission from your Lord (Almighty and Glorious is He)."

> While he is standing at the entrance to the Garden of Paradise, he will catch sight of the occupants of the Fire of Hell. He will also hear them howling like dogs, so he will weep as he pleads: "O my Lord, turn my face away from the people of the Fire of Hell. I shall never ask You, O my Lord, for any other favour!"
>
> That same angel will then come to him from the presence of the Lord of All the Worlds (Almighty and Glorious is He). The angel will move his face away from the Fire of Hell, and turn it around towards the Garden of Paradise.

From the same traditional report, transmitted on the authority of Abū Huraira (may Allāh be well pleased with him), we learn that Allāh's Messenger (Allāh bless him and give him peace) went on to say:

> The spot where that man is obliged to stand and wait will be no more than a footstep away from the entrance to the Garden of Paradise, so he will find himself looking directly at the door of the Garden of Paradise. As he surveys its width, he will discover that the two side-posts of the door of the Garden of Paradise are very far apart – so far apart, in fact, that even the swiftest of birds would take forty years to fly from one of them to the other.
>
> That man will then make a request of his Lord (Almighty and Glorious is He), to whom he will say: "O my Lord, You have indeed treated me with the utmost kindness. You have delivered me from the Fire of Hell, and You have averted my face from the inhabitants of the Fire of Hell and turned it towards the Garden of Paradise. Between me and the door of the Garden of Paradise there is now but a single footstep, so I beg You, O my Lord, through Your Might and Glory, to let me enter the door! I shall not ask You for anything other than this. But do place a screen between me and the inhabitants of

> the Fire of Hell, so that I cannot hear the dreadful hissing sound it constantly emits, and so that I cannot see its occupants.
>
> That same angel will then come to him again from the presence of the Lord of All the Worlds (Almighty and Glorious is He). "O son of Adam," the angel will say, "you are so untrue to your word! Did you not insist that you would not ask for anything else?"
>
> The man will respond to this reproach by swearing: "No, by the Might and Glory of the Lord, I shall not ask for anything else!" The angel will thereupon take him by the hand and cause him to enter the door. Then the angel will fly away, returning to the presence of the Lord of All the Worlds (Almighty and Glorious is He).

The Prophet (Allāh bless him and give him peace) continued:

> Now that he is inside the Garden of Paradise, that man will look to his right and to his left, as well as to his front, scanning an area that extends to the distance of a whole year's journey, yet he will not see anyone there. In all that space, he will see nothing but trees and fruit, and the nearest tree will be just one footstep away from the spot on which he is standing.
>
> As he looks at that tree, he will notice that its trunk is of gold and its branches of bright silver, that its leaves are like the finest ornaments any human being ever saw, that its fruits are creamier than butter and sweeter than honey, and that its aroma is more fragrant than musk.
>
> That man will be utterly bewildered by all the sights he sees. He will therefore say: "O my Lord, You have delivered me from Hell [*Jahannam*] and allowed me to enter the door of the Garden of Paradise, so You

have treated me with the utmost kindness. The distance between me and this tree is merely that of a single footstep; I shall ask You for nothing else, apart from permission to take that one step!"

That same angel will thereupon come to him and say: "You are so untrue to your word, O son of Adam! Did you not insist that you would not ask for anything more?" So what do you mean by making this extra request, and what has become of the solemn oath you swore? Do you not feel any sense of shame?"

The angel will thereupon take him by the hand and transport him to the least imposing of all the dwellings assigned to him. To his amazement, he will find this to be a palatial mansion, built of pearls, that stretches before him to the distance of a full year's journey.

As soon as he arrives there, however, and surveys the scene in front of him, he will find himself looking at another dwelling place, at which point that pearly mansion – along with everything else that is now behind him – will seem to him like no more than a dream. Once he has seen it, he will be unable to control himself, so he will say: "O my Lord, I am asking You to grant me this dwelling, and I shall not ask You for anything else!"

One of the angels will thereupon come to him and say: "O son of Adam, did you not commit yourself to the solemn oath you swore by your Lord? You are so untrue to your word, O son of Adam! Nevertheless, the dwelling is yours." As soon as he arrives there, however, and surveys the scene in front of him, he will find himself looking at yet another dwelling place, at which point the previous one will seem to him like no more than a dream. So he will say: "O my Lord, I am asking You to grant me this dwelling!"

That same angel will thereupon come to him and say: "O son of Adam, what is the matter with you? Do you never fulfil a solemn vow? Did you not insist that you would not ask for anything else?" Nevertheless, the angel will not reproach him too severely, because it will be quite obvious to him that the poor man is almost beside himself through being exposed to such marvels and wonders. So the angel will tell him: "It is yours!"

The Prophet (Allāh bless him and give him peace) continued:

At this point, yet another dwelling place will suddenly appear in front of him, and those he saw previously will seem to him like no more than a dream. He will therefore be left flabbergasted, too dumbfounded to express himself in coherent speech.

Allāh's Messenger (Allāh bless him and give him peace) will then say to him: "What is the matter with you now? Have you no request to make of your Lord?"

Recovering his power of speech, the man will reply: "O my master, may Allāh bless you [*yā sayyidī, ṣalla 'llāhu ʿalaik*]! By Allāh, I have already given my oath to the Lord of Might and Glory [*Rabb al-ʿIzza*] on so many occasions that I now feel afraid of Him, I have asked Him for so much that I now feel a sense of shame."

At this point, the Lord of Might and Glory (Magnificent is His Majesty) will say to the man: "Will it please you if I gather the whole world – from the day when I created it till the day when I caused it to be no more – and put it all together for your sake, then multiply it ten times over for your benefit?"

That man will respond to this by saying: "O my Lord, can You be making fun of me, when You are the Lord of All the Worlds?" The Lord of Might and Glory (Majestic and Exalted is He) will then say to the man: "I am indeed Capable of doing it, so ask Me for whatever you wish!"

At this point, the man will say: "O my Lord, allow me to join the company of human beings!"

An angel will thereupon come and take him by the hand, then walk with him into the Garden of Paradise, until something becomes apparent to him – something the like of which he has never seen. At the sight of this apparition, he will immediately prostrate himself, saying in his posture of prostration: "My Lord (Almighty and Glorious is He) has manifested Himself to me!" The angel will then say to him: "Lift up your head. This is your dwelling place, although it is only the least of your dwellings."

The man will then say: "If Allāh (Almighty and Glorious is He) had not made me close my eyes, they would have been completely dazzled by the radiant light of this palatial mansion."

While the man is proceeding to make himself at home in that palatial mansion, another man will come to meet him. At the sight of this person's face and clothing, he will be rendered speechless with astonishment, thinking that his visitor must be an angel. The newcomer will approach him, saying: "Peace be upon you, and Allāh's mercy and blessings [*as-salāmu ʿalaika wa raḥmatu 'llāhi wa barakātuh*]! This is just the right moment for you to arrive here!" The first man will return his greeting of peace, then ask him: "Who are you, O servant of Allāh?" The other will reply: "I am a steward [*qahramān*] at your service. I have been appointed to manage this particular household, but you also have at your disposal a thousand other stewards like me, each of them in charge of one of your palatial mansions. You have a thousand palatial mansions in your possession, each with a staff of one thousand servants, as well as wives from among the brides of Paradise with those lovely eyes of theirs [*al-ḥūr al-ʿīn*]."

On entering that palatial mansion of his, the man will discover that it has a dome, which has been carved out of a single pearl. He will find that there are seventy apartments inside the hollow interior of the dome, with seventy rooms inside each apartment. On closer inspection, he will notice that each room has seventy doors, and that each of those doors is equipped with its own dome of pearls. When he enters those domes, he will be the very first person to open them, since they have never been opened previously by any of Allāh's creatures.

At a certain point during his tour of the hollow interior of that great dome, lo and behold, he will suddenly find himself inside a dome that has been carved out of a precious red stone. It is seventy cubits in height, and has seventy doors. Each of those doors leads through to a precious stone, of similar height and likewise equipped with seventy doors. None of the precious stones is of the same colour as the one next to it. Inside each of the precious stones there are spouses, bridal thrones [*manāṣṣ*], and raised couches.

On entering the jewelled dome, the man will find a wife waiting there to receive him – one of the brides of Paradise with those lovely eyes of theirs [*al-ḥūr al-ʿīn*]. She will greet him at once with the Islāmic salutation, and he will give her the greeting of peace in return, but

> then he will stand rooted to the spot, too stunned to say another word. To put him at his ease, she will therefore say to him: "This is just the right time for you to visit us. I am your wife!"
>
> When he looks into her face, the man will see his own face in hers, just as one of you might look at your face in the mirror, and see the reflection of its handsome features, its beauty and its fair complexion. She is decked out with seventy articles of clothing, each of them adorned with seventy colours, of which no two are alike. When looking at her from behind, he can see the calf of her leg. Whenever he moves to view her from a different angle, she becomes seventy times more beautiful in his eyes, for she is a mirror to him, and he is a mirror to her.

From the same traditional report, transmitted on the authority of Abū Huraira (may Allāh be well pleased with him), we learn that Allāh's Messenger (Allāh bless him and give him peace) went on to say:

> Each of those palatial mansions will be equipped with three hundred and sixty doors, and each of those three hundred and sixty doors will be surmounted by a dome made from a pearl, a sapphire, and some other kind of gem. None of those domes will be of the same colour as the one next to it. When the owner surveys the area that stretches into the distance behind his palatial mansion, he will be viewing his own estate as far as his eye can see. When he sets out on a journey into that area, he will travel through his own estate for a hundred years, making a thorough inspection of everything he comes across along the way.
>
> Whenever he takes up residence in one of his palatial mansions, the angels will come in to visit him through each and every gate, bearing the greeting of peace [*salām*] and bringing him gifts from

the presence of the Lord of All the Worlds. Not one of those angels will come without bringing a set of gifts, and those gifts will always be different from the presents brought by any other angel. Every day, and all day long, the angels will come to salute him with the greeting of peace, and they will come bearing gifts. The proof of this is recorded in the Book of Allāh (Almighty and Glorious is He), for He tells us:

> *wa 'l-malā'ikatu yadkhulūna ʿalai-him min kulli bāb: salāmun ʿalai-kum bi-ma ṣabartum fa-niʿma ʿuqba 'd-dār.*
>
> **And the angels will enter unto them by every gate, [saluting them with]: "Peace be upon you, because You persevered with patience." Fair indeed is the Ultimate Abode! (13:23-24)**

He has also told us (Exalted is He):

> *wa la-hum rizqu-hum fī-hā bukratan wa ʿashiyyā.*
>
> **And there they shall have their sustenance in the early morning and in the evening. (19:62)**

According to Abū Huraira (may Allāh be well pleased with him), the Prophet (Allāh bless him and give him peace) also used to say:

> This man will be referred to as "that poor fellow" by the other inhabitants of the Garden of Paradise, on account of the superiority of their dwelling places over his, in spite of the fact that the "poor fellow" will have eighty thousand servants to wait on him at mealtimes! Whenever he feels an appetite for food, those servants will respond to his need by setting up one of the tables they keep ready for use on such occasions. The top slab of each of those tables is made from a red sapphire or ruby [*yāqūta ḥamrā'*], set in a yellow sapphire or topaz [*yāqūta ṣafrā'*], with a rim of pearls, sapphires and chrysolite or peridot [*zabarjad*]. The legs of each table are made from pearls, and they have a circumference of twenty miles.

As soon as this table has been set up, seventy different kinds of food will be laid out upon it, all for him to choose from. Eighty servants will be standing in front of him, ready to wait upon him. Each of those servants will be holding a plate of food and a glass containing something to drink. The food on each plate will be quite different from that on any other plate, and the drink in each glass will be quite different from that in any other glass. He will find the first to be just as tasty as the last, and he will find the last to be just as delicious as the first. He will compare them one with another, and he will not fail to sample each and every kind of food and drink.

As far as the servants are concerned, every single one of them will be given his fair share of that food and drink, once it has been removed from the master's presence. Besides, there will not be a single one of them who does not have seventy-two wives from among the brides of Paradise with those lovely eyes of theirs [*al-ḥūr al-ʿīn*] as well as two human wives [*ādamiyyatān*]. Each of those wives will have a palatial mansion, built from a green sapphire set inside a red one. There will be seventy thousand door panels in each of those palatial mansions, and each door panel will have its own dome, carved out of a pearl.

Among all those wives, there will not be a single one who is not wearing seventy thousand articles of clothing, with seventy thousand colours in each article of clothing, and none of those articles of clothing will resemble any other. Among all those wives, furthermore, there will not be a single one who does not have a thousand maidservants in front of her, standing ready to attend to her needs, as well as seventy thousand maidservants to wait upon her in her private sitting room. Among all those maidservants, there will not be a single one whom she does not keep actively employed in attending to her needs. Whenever a meal has been prepared for

> her, seventy thousand maidservants will stand in front of her, each of them holding a plate of food and a glass containing something to drink, and none of these offerings will be like any other.
>
> The man may find himself longing to see a brother of his, someone he used to love for the sake of Allāh (Almighty and Glorious is He) during his life in the world below. Prompted by concern for his brother's welfare, and fearing that he may have perished, the man will say: "I wish I knew what my brother So-and-So has been doing!" Allāh (Almighty and Glorious is He) will be fully aware of what is in his heart, so He will instruct his angels by way of inspiration: "Convey this servant of Mine to his brother!" One of the angels will thereupon bring him a thoroughbred riding camel, saddled and padded with blankets of light.

The Prophet (Allāh bless him and give him peace) continued:

> The angel will salute him with the greeting of peace, so he will greet him with peace [*as-salām*] in return. Then the angel will tell him: "Get up and mount this camel! Away you go to find your brother!"
>
> The man will then proceed to mount the camel, and so he will set out on a journey through the Garden of Paradise. The distance he has to travel would take a thousand years on this earth, but he will cover it in less time than one of you would take to mount a thoroughbred camel and ride it for just one league [*farsakh*].[23]
>
> Nothing will happen to him until he reaches the home of his brother. He will thereupon salute him with the greeting of peace, and his brother will greet him with peace [*as-salām*] in return, as he assures

23 The *farsakh* [parasang, or league] is three miles of the Hāshimī measure, i.e. thirty bow-shots reckoning the bow-shot as four hundred cubits, or sixty bow-shots reckoning the bow shot as two hundred cubits. (See E.W. Lane, *Arabic-English Lexicon*, art. *F-R-S-KH*)

him that he is a very welcome guest. He will then say: "Where have you been, O my brother? I have been so concerned about you!"

Each of them will thereupon embrace the other, then both of them will say: "Praise be to Allāh, the One who has brought us together again!" The pair of them will go on praising Allāh (Almighty and Glorious is He) in the most beautiful voices ever heard by any human being.

At this point, Allāh (Almighty and Glorious is He) will say to them: "O you two servants of Mine, this is not the time for serious work. This is rather the time for cheerful greetings and requests, so put your requests to Me, and I shall grant you both whatever you wish." In response to this offer, the pair of them will say: "O Lord, allow us to be together in this station [of Paradise]!"

Allāh (Almighty and Glorious is He) will therefore cause that station [of Paradise] to be the place where they can settle down and make themselves at home [*majlis*], in a tent encased in pearls and sapphires. Their wives will also be given a similar dwelling place, and so they will all proceed to drink, eat, and enjoy themselves.

As soon as one of the men in the Garden of Paradise has taken a morsel of food and put it in his mouth, it may occur to him that he actually fancies a different kind of food. If this should happen, the morsel concerned would immediately change into whatever he really wanted to eat!

According to the same traditional report, transmitted on the authority of Abū Huraira (may Allāh be well pleased with him), somebody once asked: "O Messenger of Allāh, what makes up the ground of the Garden of Paradise?"

To this he replied (Allāh bless him and give him peace):

Its ground is a kind of marble or alabaster slab [*rukhāma*] consisting of smooth silver, and its dust consists of musk. Its hills are of saffron, and its walls are made of pearls and sapphires, as well as of gold and silver. The outside of the walls can be seen from the area inside them, and their interior is likewise visible from their exterior. In the whole of the Garden of Paradise, there is not one palatial mansion of which the exterior is not visible from the interior, and the interior from the exterior.

In the whole of the Garden of Paradise, furthermore, there will not be one man who is not dressed in a waist-wrapper [*izār*], an upper-body shawl [*ridā'*], and other garments, not one of which has been cut, and not one of which has been sewn. Nor will there be one man among them who is not wearing a crown, hollowed out of a large pearl, and studded with smaller pearls, sapphires, and chrysolite or peridot [*zabarjad*].[24] He will have two plaited strands [*ḍafīratān*] of gold in his hair, and around his neck he will wear a collar of gold, encased in pearls and green sapphires. On the wrist of each and every man amongst them there will be three bracelets: a bracelet of gold, a bracelet of silver, and a bracelet of pearl. Beneath their crowns there will be diadems of pearls and sapphires. Over those garments of theirs they will be wearing fine silk brocade [*sundus*], and over that fine silk brocade there will also be thick silk brocade interwoven with gold [*istabraq*], as well as plain green silk.

As for the cushions on which the people of the Garden of Paradise will be reclining in the greatest comfort, their inner surfaces consist

24 The principal Arabic-English dictionaries give chrysolite as the meaning of *zabarjad*. According to *Webster's Ninth New Collegiate Dictionary*, chrysolite or olivine is "a usually greenish mineral, that is a complex silicate of magnesium and iron, used esp. in refractories," while peridot is "a deep yellowish green transparent olivine used as a gem."

> of thick silk brocade interwoven with gold [*istabraq*], and their outer surfaces of beautiful multicoloured carpeting [*ʿabqarī*]. The cushions are laid on raised couches, made of red sapphire, and these have pearls as their supports. Each and every one of those raised couches has a thousand decorative patterns, with seventy colours to each pattern, and no two patterns are alike. Seventy thousand rugs are spread out in front of each of those raised couches, with seventy colours to each rug, and not one of those rugs bears any resemblance to the one beside it. To the right of each of those raised couches there are seventy thousand pedestals, with an equal number to the left, and not one of those pedestals is similar to any other.

According to Abū Huraira (may Allāh be well pleased with him), the Prophet (Allāh bless him and give him peace) also used to say:

> The people of the Garden of Paradise in their entirety, the loftiest of them and the lowliest of them in spiritual rank, will be of the same physical height as Adam, and the physical height of Adam (peace be upon him) is sixty cubits [*dhirāʿ*]. They will all be youthful, devoid of bodily and facial hair, anointed with kohl[25] and lined with charcoal around the eyes – they and their womenfolk to exactly the same extent.

When they have received all the special treatment thus far described, a herald will utter a proclamation within the Garden of Paradise. Raising his voice so that it can be heard by those at the loftiest and the lowliest levels, by those who are nearest to him, and by those who are farthest away, the herald will cry: "O people of the Garden of Paradise, are you pleased with your dwelling places?" To this they will all reply in chorus: "Yes, by Allāh! Our Lord has now caused us

---

25 Kohl (from the Arabic word *kuḥl*) is a powder, usually a preparation of pulverised antimony, used for darkening the edges of the eyelids.

to dwell in the dwelling place of dignity and honour. We have no desire for any change of location, nor do we wish for any substitute instead of it. We are well pleased with our Lord as a neighbour! O Allāh, our Lord, we have listened to Your herald, and we have given him an honest reply. O Allāh, our Lord, we yearned to look upon Your countenance, and You showed it to us for that, as You surely knew, would be the most excellent part of our reward."

The Prophet (Allāh bless him and give him peace) continued:

At this point, Allāh (Almighty and Glorious is He) will give an order to the particular Garden of Paradise in which He has His dwelling [*manzil*] and His seat [*majlis*]. He will tell that Garden, the name of which is the Abode of Peace [*Dār as-Salām*]: "Gather up all your finery and make yourself really beautiful! Make yourself ready for the visit of My servants!" She will listen intently to her Lord, and will obey Him even before the word of command has been completely expressed. She will immediately gather up all her finery, and make herself ready to receive the visitors of Allāh (Exalted is He), whereupon Allāh (Exalted is He) will give the order to one of the angels: "Invite My servants to come and visit Me!"

That angel will promptly set forth from the presence of the All-Merciful One [*ar-Raḥmān*], in order to proclaim this invitation at the top of his voice. In a deliciously sweet and drawn out voice, peculiar to himself alone, the angel will say: "O people of the Garden of Paradise! O saintly friends [*awliyā*ʾ] of Allāh! Come visit your Lord!"

The sound of the angel's voice will thus be heard by the loftiest and the lowliest of the inhabitants of the Garden of Paradise, so all of them will mount up on riding beasts, whether they be she-camels or plain old nags. Keeping to the shady side, they will ride towards hills of white musk and yellow saffron. Then, when they reach the entrance [to the Abode of Peace], they will utter a special form of salutation. In expressing this salutation [*taslīm*] of theirs, they will say: "Peace be upon us from our Lord [*as-salāmu ʿalai-nā min Rabbi-nā*]!" Then they will seek permission to enter, and permission will be granted to them, so they will move straight ahead and go in through the gate.

At this point, a wind will blow forth from beneath the Heavenly Throne, the name of it being The Whirlwind [*al-Muthīra*]. It will pulverise the hills of musk and saffron, filling the people's collars and sleeves with dust, and heaping dust on their heads and over their clothes. Thus they will enter [the Abode of Peace]. As they look towards the Throne [*ʿArsh*] of their Lord and His Footstool [*Kursī*], they will see a bright light beaming at them, but without His making Himself clearly manifest to them, so they will say "Glory be to You, our Lord Most Holy [*Subḥāna-ka Rabba-nā Quddūs*], Lord of the Angels and of the Spirit [*Rabb al-Malāʾikati wa 'r-Rūḥ*]. Blessed and Exalted are You [*tabārakta wa taʿālait*]! Allow us to see, so that we may look upon Your countenance!"

In response to this plea, Allāh (Almighty and Glorious is He) will give the order to the veils, which are made of light: "Remove yourselves!" Without interruption, one veil after another will thereupon withdraw itself, until seventy veils have withdrawn themselves - each veil being seventy times more intensely radiant than its predecessor - at which point the Lord of Might and Glory (Almighty and Majestic is He) will manifest Himself to them in perfect clarity. They will at once fall down in abject prostration before Him, to remain in that posture for as long as Allāh wills. While they are still prostrating themselves, they will say: "Glory be to You! To You be the praise and the glorification [*tasbīḥ*] forever and ever! You have delivered us from the Fire of Hell, and You have caused us to enter the Garden of Paradise. Good indeed is the abode! We are utterly and completely content with You, so be well pleased with us!"

Allāh (Blessed and Exalted is He) will respond to this by saying: "I am indeed well pleased with you, to the fullest extent. But this is not the appropriate time for serious work. This is rather the time for refreshment and blissful happiness, so ask of Me and I shall grant your requests, and make your wishes known to Me, for then I shall give you even more."

Thus they will make their dearest wishes known, although they will do so without having to say a word. They will all have the same wish in common, namely that He should allow them to keep what He has given them on a permanent basis. He will therefore say to them (Exalted is He): "I shall indeed allow you to keep what I have given you on a permanent basis, and the same applies to all the extra blessings I have bestowed upon you!"

On hearing this promise from their Lord, they will raise their heads at once, as they utter the affirmation of the Supreme Greatness of Allāh [*at-takbīr*].[26] They will be not be capable, however, of raising their eyes directly towards their Lord (Almighty and Glorious is He), due to the extreme intensity of the Light of the Lord of Might and Glory [*Nūr Rabb al-ʿIzza*]. (By the way, that reception room [*majlis*] is called the East Wing of the Dome of the Throne of the Lord of All the Worlds [*Sharqī Qubbat ʿArsh Rabb al-ʿĀlamīn*].) The Lord of Might and Glory will say to them: "Welcome, O My servants. My neighbours, My chosen ones, My dear ones, My saintly friends [*awliyāʾ-ī*], the best I have among all My creatures, and My obedient people!"

---

26 That is to say, they will exclaim: "*Allāhu Akbar* [Allāh is Supremely Great!]"

> Pulpits of light will suddenly appear in front of the Throne of the Lord of Might and Glory; beneath those pulpits, chairs of light; beneath those chairs, cushions; beneath those cushions, padded quilts; and beneath those padded quilts, carpets.
>
> The Lord of Might and Glory will then say to them: "Come, seat yourselves according to your honour and nobility." So the Messengers [*Rusul*] will come forward and seat themselves upon those pulpits, while the Prophets [*Anbiyā'*] come forward and seat themselves upon those chairs, and the righteous [*ṣāliḥūn*] come forward and seat themselves upon those carpets. Tables of light will then be set up for their benefit, each table being adorned with seventy different colours, and crowned with an array of pearls and sapphires.

The Prophet (Allāh bless him and give him peace) went on to say:

> The Lord of Might and Glory will then say to His helpers [*ḥafada*]: "Give them cooked food to eat!" Seventy thousand dishes, made from pearls and sapphires, will at once be set out for them on each and every table, with each and every dish containing seventy different kinds of cooked food.
>
> The Lord of Might and Glory will then say to them: "Eat up, O My servants!" So they will eat as much of all that as Allāh wills. They will say to one another: "The food we are enjoying today is so special! The meals we used to eat, at home with our families, seem like nothing but a dream by comparison!"
>
> The Lord of Might and Glory will then say to His helpers [*ḥafada*]: "Now give My servants something to quench their thirst!" Obedient to His command, the helpers will at once provide the servants of their Lord with a thirst-quenching beverage, and they will drink

from it, saying to one another as they do so: "By comparison with the drink we can now enjoy, what we used to drink seems like nothing but a dream!"

The Lord of Might and Glory will then say to His helpers [*ḥafada*]: "You have supplied them with cooked food, and you have given them plenty to drink, so now you must provide them with fruit for their dessert!" Obedient to His command, the helpers will at once provide the servants of their Lord with fruit for their dessert. While eating it, they will say to one another: "By comparison with what we are now enjoying for dessert, the fruit we used to eat seems like nothing but a dream!"

The Lord of Might and Glory will then say to His helpers [*ḥafada*]: "You have supplied them with cooked food, you have given them plenty to drink, and you have provided them with fruit for their dessert, so now you must equip them with fine clothes and adornments." Obedient to His command, the helpers will at once produce fine clothes and adornments for the servants of their Lord to wear. As they are dressing themselves up in them, they will say to one another: "By comparison with all this finery, our previous clothing and adornments seem like nothing but a dream!"

Then, while they are still sitting in their seats, Allāh (Almighty and Glorious is He) will send forth, from beneath His Throne, a wind that is called The Whirlwind [*al-Muthīra*]. As it blows towards them with a cloud of musk and camphor – whiter than snow – from beneath the Throne, this wind will deposit a gentle dust upon their robes and their heads, as well as inside their collars and sleeves, fragrantly perfuming them in the process. The tables will then be removed from their presence, along with whatever is left of the food spread out upon them.

At this point, the Lord of Might and Glory will say to them: "Ask of Me now, for I shall grant your requests, and make your wishes known to Me, for I shall give you even more!" They will all respond to this together, saying in chorus: "O Allāh, our Lord, what we ask of You is that You should be well pleased with us!" So He will say (Almighty and Glorious is He): "I have indeed already come to be well pleased with you, O My servants!"

The Prophet (Allāh bless him and give him peace) continued further:

On hearing these words of acceptance from their Lord, they will at once bow down in abject prostration before Him, proclaiming His Glory and His Supreme Greatness [*bi 't-tasbīḥ wa 't-takbīr*][27] as they do so. The Lord of Might and Glory will then say to them: "O My servants, lift up your heads! This is not the appropriate time for serious work. This is rather the time for refreshment and blissful happiness."

They will therefore lift up their heads, with their faces glowing from the Light of their Lord. The Lord of Might and Glory (Almighty and Majestic is He) will then say to them: "Now depart to your dwellings!" They will thereupon go forth from the presence of their Lord. Then their youthful attendants will come to meet them, bringing their riding beasts.

Thus each and every one amongst them will mount his she-camel or his plain old nag, and seventy thousand youthful attendants will mount up beside him, on the same kind of animal as the one he is riding. If any of them wishes to make his way home separately, he will set off accordingly, then the rest of them will travel together, until one of their number approaches the palatial mansion that represents his destination.

27 That is to say, they will exclaim: "*Subḥāna 'llāh* [Glory be to Allāh!]"and "*Allāhu Akbar* [Allāh is Supremely Great!]"

As soon as one of them reaches his own palatial mansion, and enters the presence of his wife, she will arise to greet him and bid him welcome. She will say to him: "You have come back home to me, O my darling! You have come back home to me – and with so much more than you had, when I saw you leave on your trip! You have grown more handsome than ever. You have acquired an even greater radiance and beauty. You are wearing splendid new clothes, a fresh perfume, and so much finery!"

At this point an angel will issue a proclamation from the presence of the All-Merciful One [*ar-Raḥmān*] (Almighty and Glorious is He), crying out in a very loud voice: "O people of the Garden of Paradise, that is how it will always be for you, as your state of bliss is constantly renewed for your benefit!"

[In the words of Allāh (Almighty and Glorious is He)]:

wa 'l-malā'ikatu yadkhulūna 'alai-him min kulli bāb: salāmun 'alai-kum bi-ma ṣabartum Fa-ni'ma 'uqba 'd-dār.

And the angels will enter unto them by every gate, [saluting them with]: "Peace be upon you, because You persevered with patience." Fair indeed is the Ultimate Abode! (13:23-24)

Your Lord will surely pronounce the greeting of peace upon you, and you will be provided with many kinds of food and drink, as well as clothing and finery.

According to Abū Huraira (may Allāh be well pleased with him), the Prophet (Allāh bless him and give him peace) also used to say:

In the Garden of Paradise there are one hundred ascending stages [*mi'a daraja*]. Between each two stages there is a commanding officer

> [*amīr*], who is viewed by the inhabitants as worthy of respect, and as fit to exercise authority.
>
> The Garden of Paradise contains mountains of white musk and yellow saffron, the effects of which are highly beneficial to the inhabitants. When they eat their food, the gas they expel from their stomachs is even more fragrant than musk. When they drink their pure wine, their skins simply perspire. They do not evacuate their bowels, nor do they urinate. They do not spit, nor do they blow their noses. They do not fall sick, nor do they suffer from headaches.

According to Abū Huraira (may Allāh be well pleased with him), the Prophet (Allāh bless him and give him peace) also used to say:

> The people of the Garden of Paradise, the loftiest and the lowliest of them alike, spend their time as follows: They start the clay by reclining in comfort for two hours, then they indulge for two hours in friendly competition [*wa yatafāḍalūna*].[28] After praising their Creator [*Khāliq*] for the next four hours, they spend two hours visiting with one another.
>
> There are times of night and day in the Garden of Paradise, and there is darkness. Its nighttime is far brighter, however, than any daytime. The day has seventy parts.
>
> As for the least well endowed of all the people of the Garden of Paradise, he is still someone who – if all of mankind and the jinn came to visit him at once – would have enough chairs, cushions, quilts and rugs for his guests to sit and recline upon, as well as

28 At this point in the Damascus edition of the Arabic text of *al-Ghunya*, the editor inserts the following footnote: "As for the use of the expression *wa yatafāḍalūna* in this context, the meaning of it needs to be investigated. It would also be advisable to check the reading of the *ḥadīth* for correctness."

enough tables, dishes, servants, food and drink to entertain them satisfactorily, if not to the same extent as the next man above him.

As for the trees in the Garden of Paradise, their trunks are mostly of gold, although some are of silver, some of sapphire, and some of chrysolite or peridot [*zabarjad*]. Their palm boughs [*saʿaf*] are constituted from the same range of materials. Their leaves are like the most beautiful articles of clothing anyone has ever seen, while their fruits are creamier than butter and sweeter than honey. The height of each of those trees is equal to the distance of a journey taking five hundred years, while its thickness at the base of the trunk is equal to the distance of a seventy-year journey.

Whenever any man amongst the inhabitants of the Garden of Paradise happens to raise his eyes, he will find himself looking at the far end of a branch of one of the trees, and at the fruits with which it is laden. He will notice that every tree bears seventy thousand types of fruit, yet no kind has quite the same taste and flavour as any other. If he feels a desire to sample one of those many varieties, the branch that carries the particular fruit he fancies will bend down towards him – from the distance of a journey taking five hundred years, or fifty years, or less than that – so that he may pick the fruit with his hand, if he wishes to do so. If it is not convenient for him to pick it with his hand, he has only to open his mouth, for the fruit will simply drop into his open mouth. As soon as any item is harvested from those fruit trees, Allāh will immediately create something even finer and tastier to take its place. Then, once the man has picked all the fruit he needs to satisfy his appetite, the bough will return to its previous position.

There is one tree that does not bear fruit. It is laden instead with spathes or envelopes [*akmām*] containing unembroidered silk, articles of clothing, silk brocade [*sundus*], ornaments, and fine carpets [*ʿabqarī*]. There is also one tree amongst them that bears spathes containing musk and camphor.

According to Abū Huraira (may Allāh be well pleased with him), the Prophet (Allāh bless him and give him peace) also used to say:

The people of the Garden of Paradise will behold their Lord every Friday [the Day of Congregational Prayer].

If a diadem [*iklīl*] from the Garden of Paradise were ever to be sent down from heaven above, the light of the sun would disappear.

There are certain palatial mansions in the Garden of Paradise, each of which has four streams inside it: water from a spring, milk from a spring, wine from a spring, and honey from a spring. If someone drinks any part of this, the taste it leaves behind will prove to be the flavour of musk [*ṣāra khitāmu-hu miskan*].[29]

They will not drink anything from it until it has been blended in a mixture from the fountains of the Garden of Paradise, one of which is known as *az-Zanjabīl* [Ginger],[30] another as

29 An allusion to the verse [*āya*] of the Qurʾān in which Allāh (Almighty and Glorious is He) has told us, with reference to a pure wine given to the righteous to drink in the Garden of Paradise: *khitāmu-hu misk.* **Its end result shall be the taste of musk. (83:26)**

30 This statement attributed to the Prophet (Allāh bless him and give him peace) lends support to the view of those authorities who take *Zanjabīl* to be another name for *Salsabīl*, the fountain from which the wine of Paradise is drawn. As we read in the Qurʾān: *wa yusqawna fī-hā kaʾsan kāna mizāju-hā zanjabīlā: ʿainan fī-hā tusammā Salsabīlā.* **And therein they shall be given to drink a cup whose mixture is *zanjabīl*, a spring therein, named *Salsabīl*. (76:17-18)** Some commentators understand this to mean that the wine of the fountain will have the aromatic flavour of ginger. According to the classical Arabic lexicographers, *zanjabīl* [ginger; the root of the ginger plant] "has a property that is warming, digestive, lenitive in a small degree, strengthening to the venereal faculty, clearing to the phlegm, sharpening to the intellect and exhilarating." (See: E.W. Lane, *Arabic-English Lexicon*, art. *Z-N-J-B-L*)

Tasnīm[31] and the other as *Kāfūr* [Camphor].[32] Those who are brought near [to the Lord] will drink a pure wine concocted from all of these.

Were it not for the fact that Allāh has passed judgement amongst them, to the effect that they must hand the goblet around from one to another, they would never let it leave their mouths.

In the course to paying visits to one another, the people of the Garden of Paradise will cover the distance of a journey taking a hundred thousand years, and even more than that. Nevertheless, when they return from visiting their brethren, they will find their way home more directly than one of you could get back to his house.

When the people of the Garden of Paradise have seen their Lord (Almighty and Glorious is He), and are ready to set out for home, every man amongst them will be given a green pomegranate [*rummāna*] containing seventy seeds. Each seed will have seventy colours, and no seed will be of quite the same sort as any other. Then, as they make their departure from the presence of their Lord (Almighty and Glorious is He), they will pass through the markets

---

31 This foundation is mentioned in the Qur'ān in connection with the pure wine referred to in note 29 above: *wa mizāhu-hu min Tasnīm 'ainan yashrabu bi-hā 'l-muqarrabūn.* **And its mixture is from *Tasnīm*, a fountain at which those brought near [to the Lord] do drink. (83:27-29)** As an ordinary verbal noun, the Arabic word *tasnīm* means "raising something into the shape of a camel's hump [*sanām*]." According to the classical lexicographers, the fountain is called *Tasnīm* because it flows above the elevated chambers and pavilions of Paradise. (See: E.W. Lane, *Arabic-English Lexicon,* art. *S-N-M*)

32 The fountain called *Kāfūr* [Camphor] is also mention in the Qur'ān, where Allāh (Almighty and Glorious is He) has told us: *inna 'l-abrāra yashrabūna min ka'sin kāna mizāju-hā kāfūrā: 'ainan yashrabu bi-hā 'ibādu 'llāhi.* **Surely the pious shall drink of a cup whose mixture is camphor, a fountain at which the servants of Allāh do drink. (76:5-6)** As in the case of *Zanjabīl* [Ginger], referred to in note 30 above, the statement here attributed to the Prophet (Allāh bless him and give him peace) lends support to the view of those authorities who take *Kāfūr* [Camphor] to be the actual name of the fountain. According to some, however, notably including the distinguished commentator al-Baiḍāwī, the meaning of the Qur'ānic verse [*āya*] is that the wine of Paradise will be mixed with camphor [*kāfūr*] because of its agreeable coolness and aroma.

of the Garden of Paradise. There will be no business of buying and selling in progress in those markets, but they will be well stocked with ornamental goods, articles of clothing, silk brocade [*sundus*], thick silk brocade interwoven with gold [*istabraq*], unembroidered silk, decorative items of gold and jewellery [*zukhruf*], fine carpets [*ʿabqarī*] woven from pearls and sapphires, and diadems suspended on display. They will therefore take from those markets as many of these varied goods as they can carry with them, and yet the markets will not have their stocks diminished by as much as a single item.

The markets of the Garden of Paradise will also contain dummy figures, similar in form to the most handsome human beings in existence. The forehead of each of these dummy figures will be marked with the inscription: "If anyone wishes to have the same good looks as mine, Allāh will cause that person to become just as handsome as my shape and form." If anyone responds to this by wishing that his own face could be just as good looking as that of the dummy figure, Allāh will promptly fulfil that person's wish.

Then they will depart for their own dwelling places, and their servants will promptly line up in rows to meet them, standing to attention in order to bid them welcome and greet them with the salutation of peace. Each of them will engage in cheerful conversation with the companion who is travelling with him, until the good news of his arrival reaches his wife. She will then be so transported by joy that she will set out towards him. She will meet him at his door with a welcoming greeting and the salutation of peace. She will give him a hug and he will embrace her, and so they will go inside together, locked in a mutual embrace.

If any woman from among the womenfolk of the Garden of Paradise ever happened to come into view, no angel brought near [to the Lord] nor any Prophet sent as a Messenger [*Nabī Mursal*] who caught sight of her would fail to be enchanted by her beauty.

The last draught to be drunk by the people of the Garden of Paradise in the wake of their meal is a beverage called "pure and plentiful" [*ṭahūr dihāq*]. As soon as a draught of it has been drunk, their food and drink will be fully digested. It will cause the contents of their bellies to acquire a fragrance like that of musk. Their belching and burping will also have the scent of musk, and there will be no pain or discomfort in their bellies. When they drink, they will stimulate a healthy appetite for the meal, so this will always be their regular practice.

The riding animals of the people of the Garden of Paradise are created from white sapphire.

The Prophet (Allāh bless him and give him peace) also used to say:

There are three Gardens of Paradise: [The one known simply as] the Garden [*al-Janna*]; [The Garden of] Eden [*ʿAdn*] and The Abode of Peace [*Dār as-Salām*]. [The one known simply as] the Garden [*al-Janna*] is smaller than the Garden of Eden [*Jannat ʿAdn*] by a factor of seven hundred million.

As for the palatial mansions of the Garden, their exterior is of gold, while their interior consists of chrysolite or peridot [*zabarjad*]. Their turrets are made from red rubies, and their balconies are constructed by an arrangement of strung pearls.

The man among the people of the Garden of Paradise will enjoy reclining next to his wife for a single session lasting seven hundred years, during the whole of which time he will never once move away from her side. Then his other wife will call out to him from a palatial mansion that is even more beautiful, saying: "O my brother [in faith], the time has now come for you to let us have our turn with you!" So the man will say: "Who are you?" and she will reply: "I am part of that [consolation] to which Allāh (Almighty and Glorious is He) is referring when He says:
fa-lā taʿlamu nafsun mā ukhfiya la-hum min qurrati aʿyun: jazāʾan bi-mā kānū yaʿmalūn.
So no soul knows what comfort is kept secretly in store for them, as a reward for what they used to do. (32:17)

He will therefore move over to join her, and he will continue to reside with her for a period of seven hundred years, eating and drinking in her company and having sexual intercourse with her throughout that time.

In the Garden of Paradise there is a tree, in the shade of which a rider can travel for seven hundred years without ever passing beyond it. Streams flow beneath that tree, and whole cities are built upon each of its many branches. The length of each of those cities is ten thousand miles, and the distance between each city and the next is like the distance between the East and the West. The springs of the Fountain of Paradise [*Salsabīl*] flow from those palatial mansions towards those cities. A single leaf from that tree is enough to provide shade for an enormously large community.

> When a man from among the people of the Garden of Paradise enters the presence of his wife, she will say: "By the One who has so generously honoured me with you, I swear that nothing in the Garden of Paradise is more dear to me than you are!" Of course, the man will also tell his wife that he feels the same way about her.

The Prophet (Allāh bless him and give him peace) also used to say:

> In the Garden of Paradise there are things that defy all efforts to describe them, of which no conception can be formed by the hearts of the learned, of which nothing can be heard by the ears of the attentive, and in it there are things that have never been seen by the eyes of created beings.
>
> Allāh (Almighty and Glorious is He) will cause those who love one another for His sake to alight in the Garden of Eden [*Jannat ʿAdn*], where He will settle them upon a pillar made from a single red ruby, the thickness of which is equal to the distance of a journey taking seventy thousand years. From this vantage point, overlooking seventy thousand residential areas, each area having a palatial mansion, they will survey the inhabitants of the Garden. Marked in light upon their foreheads, they will bear an inscription that reads: "These are they who love one another for the sake of Allāh [*hāʾulāʾi ʾl-mutaḥābbūna fi ʾllāh*]."
>
> If one of them happens to gaze from his palace towards the inhabitants of the Garden, the radiance of his face will fill the mansions of the inhabitants of the Garden with light, just as the sun illuminates the houses of the people of the earth. The inhabitants of the Garden will then look upon his face, and they will say to one another as they do so: "This must be one of those who love one another for the sake of Allāh (Almighty and Glorious is He). See how his face is like the moon on the night when it is full!"

The handsomeness of the true specimen of manhood [*rajul*], in contrast to the handsomeness of the manservant [*khādim*] among the people of the Garden of Paradise, is like [the brilliance of] the moon on the night when it is full, in contrast to [the fainter brilliance of] the stars.

As for the womenfolk of the Garden of Paradise, they mark the end of their meal by singing in delightfully sweet and drawn-out voices: "We are the women who are everlasting, so we shall never die. We are the women who are safe and sound, so we shall never be afraid. We are the women who are satisfied, so we shall never be discontented. We are the women who are forever young, so we shall never grow senile and decrepit. We are the women who are always clothed, we shall never go naked. We are the women who are good, the women who are beautiful, the wives of a truly noble people."

As for the birds of the Garden of Paradise, each of them has seventy thousand feathers. Each of those feathers has a different colour, quite unlike that of any other. The size of each bird amongst them is a mile in width by a mile in length. Whenever the true believer [*mu'min*] desires them to provide him with something to satisfy his appetite, he has only to fetch a bird and place it inside the bowl from which he intends to eat. The bird will then flap its wings and, as it rises, seventy kinds of food will fall from it into the bowl – such as cooked fare and all sorts of other tasty morsels. The flavour of this food is more delicious than honeydew, its tenderness is softer than butter, and its whiteness is whiter than buttermilk. As soon as he has eaten some of it, the bird will flap its wings again and fly away, without shedding a single feather in the process.

So that they can always enjoy this kind of service, their birds and their riding animals are carefully tended in the pastures of the Garden of Paradise surrounding their palatial mansions.

Allāh (Exalted is He) will give the people of the Garden of Paradise signet rings of gold for them to wear, these being the signet rings of eternal life. Then He will give them signet rings made of sapphire and pearls. That will be when they visit Him in the Abode of Peace [*Dār as-Salām*].

When the people of the Garden of Paradise go to visit their Lord, they will eat and drink and thoroughly enjoy themselves.

Allāh's Messenger (Allāh bless him and give him peace) also said:

The Lord of Might and Glory [*Rabb al-ʿIzza*] (Almighty and Majestic is He) will say: "O David, extol Me with your beautiful voice!" David will then extol Him for as long as Allāh (Exalted is He) wishes this celebration of His praise to continue, so that nothing in the Garden of Paradise will miss the opportunity to hear the beauty of his voice and its delightful sweetness. Then the Lord of Might and Glory (Almighty and Majestic is He) will present them with fine clothing and adornments. Then they will depart to rejoin their wives.

Every man among the people of the Garden of Paradise has access to the benefits provided by a tree called the Tree of Bliss [*Ṭūbā*]. Whenever one of them wishes to dress himself up in clothes of extremely high quality, he has only to make his way to the Tree of Bliss [*Ṭūbā*], the spathes or envelopes [*akmām*] of which will at once be opened up for him. These wardrobes are of six different kinds, each one of them containing seventy types of clothing. No article of clothing has the same colour as any other, nor is any garment tailored from the same fabric as another. He may therefore take his pick, selecting whichever of these items he wishes to wear.

The following message is inscribed on the wives of the people of the Garden of Paradise – on the area between the throat and the breast of every woman amongst them: "You are my dearly beloved, and I am your dearly beloved [*anta ḥabībī wa ana ḥabībatu-ka*]. There is no one who could ever be a match for you, and no one who could ever take your place. For you there is no malice or deceit within my heart." The man will therefore stare at the area between his wife's throat and breast, and he will see right through to the innermost core of her being [*sawād kabidi-hā*], beyond her flesh and bones, for his innermost core is a mirror to her, and her innermost core is a mirror to him. This penetration will not do her any damage, however, except in the sense that the sapphire is 'damaged' by having a string threaded through it!

The whiteness of these ladies is like the whiteness of coral pearls, and their pure clarity is like the pure clarity of sapphires. As Allāh (Almighty and Glorious is He) has told us:
ka-anna-hunna 'l-yāqūtu wa 'l-marjān.
It is as if they were sapphires and coral pearls. (55:58)

When the people of the Garden of Paradise go riding, their mounts will be fine she-camels and plain workhorses. The hoof of one of these she-camels will make contact with the ground at the farthest point within its range of vision. In the case of that plain workhorse, the touchdown point for its hoof will also be at the farthest spot within its range of sight. These animals have been created from pearls and sapphires. The magnitude of every riding beast amongst them is seventy miles [from nose to tail]. The reins and bridles of the fine she-camels, and also those of the plain workhorses, are cords of pearls and chrysolite or peridot [*zabarjad*].

Concerning the words of Allāh (Almighty and Glorious is He), in which He has given us the following description of the people of the Garden of Paradise:

fa-waqā-humu 'llāhu sharra dhālika 'l-yawmi wa laqqā-hum naḍratan wa surūrā wa jazā-hum bi-mā ṣabarū jannatan wa ḥarīrā muttaki'īna fī-hā 'ala 'l-arā'ik: lā yarawna fī-hā shamsan wa la zamharīrā wa dāniyatan 'alai-him ẓilālu-hā wa dhullilat quṭūfu-hā tadhlīlā wa yuṭāfu 'alai-him bi-āniyatin min fiḍḍatin wa akwābin kānat qawārīrā qawārīran min fiḍḍatin qaddarū-hā taqdīrā wa yusqawna fī-hā ka'san kāna mizāju-hā zanjabīlā – 'ainan fī-hā tusammā Salsabīlā. wa yaṭūfu 'alai-him wildānun mukhalladūn: idhā ra'aita-hum ḥasibta-hum lu'lu'an manthūrā. wa idhā ra'aita thamma ra'aita na'īmān wa mulkan kabīrā. 'aliya-hum thiyābu sundusin khuḍrun wa istabraq: wa ḥullū asāwira min fiḍḍa: wa saqā-hum Rabbu-hum sharāban ṭahūrā. inna hādhā kāna la-kum jazā'an wa kāna sa'yu-kum mashkūrā.

> **Allāh has therefore warded off from them the evil of that day, and He has made them find cheerfulness and joy. And He has granted them, as a reward for all that they endured, a Garden [of Paradise] and silk attire. Reclining therein upon couches, they will experience there neither [the fierce heat of] a sun nor bitter cold. And close upon them is the shade thereof, while its clustered fruits bow down low. And goblets of silver are brought around for them, and vessels as clear as crystal, crystal-clear vessels made of silver, which they have measured exactly to the measure [of their own deeds]. And in it their thirst is quenched with a cup the mixture of which is *zanjabīl* [ginger], a fountain therein, named *Salsabīl.* And waiting on them are immortal youths whom, if you could see them, you would take for scattered pearls. And when you see, there you will see a state of bliss and a high estate. Their raiment will be fine green silk and gold brocade. They will be adorned with bracelets of silver, their Lord will slake their thirst with a pure drink. [And it will be said unto them]: "Behold, this is a reward for you. Your endeavour [upon earth] has found acceptance." (76:11-22)**

As for His words (Almighty and Glorious is He):

> *fa-waqā humu 'llāhu sharra dhālika 'l-yawmi...*
>
> **Allāh has therefore warded off from them the evil of that day... (76:11)**

– what He means is that, on the Day of Resurrection [*Yawm al-Qiyāma*], He will spare them from having to experience the awful intensity of the Reckoning [*Ḥisāb*] and the dread terror of Hell [*Jahannam*].

[As we know from traditional accounts, attributed to the Prophet (Allāh bless him and give him peace) and transmitted on the authority of Abū Huraira (may Allāh be well pleased with him):]

When Hell is brought forth upon the parade grounds of the Resurrection [*ʿaraṣāt al-Qiyāma*], it will be led there by nineteen keepers from among the angels. Each and every one of those keepers will be accompanied by seventy thousand other angels, serving as his assistants, all of them rough, stern, their teeth grimly gritted, their eyes like live coals, and their colours like the flames of fire. While their nostrils give vent to lofty columns of flame and smoke, they stand at the ready, prepared at all times to receive and carry out the command of the All-Compelling One [*al-Jabbār*] (Blessed and Exalted is He).

Each keeper and his assistants will thus drag Hell along by means of a shackle and an enormous chain, sometimes walking to the right of it, sometimes to the left of it, and sometimes following up behind it. Each and every angel amongst them will hold in his hand a grappling hook made of iron. They will shout and bellow as they goad Hell along, but its slow progress will be made to the accompaniment of moaning and sighing, staggering and stumbling, clouds of gloom and smoke, rattling and clanking noises, and a towering inferno stoked by the fury of its rage against its own inhabitants. Thus they will eventually install it in a position midway between the Garden of Paradise and the place where the resurrected creatures are kept standing [*al-mawqif*].

At this point, Hell will lift its gaze. As soon as it spies the creatures assembled there, it will bolt towards them in order to devour them. Its keepers will have to pull on its chains to hold it in check, for if it were left to its own devices, it would pounce upon every believer [*muʾmin*] and unbeliever [*kāfir*] without distinction. Once it sees that it has been effectively restrained from attacking the assembled throng of creatures, it will simmer and boil with an intensity that can hardly be distinguished from the most furious kind of rage. Then it will heave another sigh, and the resurrected creatures will hear the sound of the gnashing of its teeth. This will cause their hearts to shudder and tremble with alarm. They will fly into a state of panic, their eyes will glaze over, and their hearts will end up in their throats.

Then Hell will heave a deep sigh, which will so affect those who hear it that not a single one of them will fail to sink down on his knees – not one angel brought near to the Lord [*mal'ak muqarrab*], not one Prophet sent as a Messenger [*Nabī Mursal*], and not one of those resurrected creatures who are present at the place of standing [*al-mawqif*].

Then Hell will heave a second deep sigh, and not a single eye that still has a drop of moisture in it will fail to shed a tear.

Then Hell will heave a third deep sigh, and even if those who hear that sigh – be they human beings or jinn – were each endowed with the merit of seventy-two Prophets, they would surely suppose that they must be embracing her as a man embraces a woman [*la-ẓannū anna-hum muwāqiʿū-hā*],[33] and that they could not possibly escape from her embrace.

Then Hell will heave a fourth deep sigh, and nothing that is capable of speech will fail to have its speech arrested. The only exceptions will be Gabriel, Michael, and [Abraham] the Bosom Friend [*Khalīl*] of the All-Merciful One [*ar-Raḥmān*] (Almighty and Glorious is He), each one of whom

33 In a previous subsection of the Discourse, where this account of Hell's appearance at the Resurrection is attributed to the Prophet (Allāh bless him and give him peace), the wording is slightly different at this point. In the passage translated on page 23 above, the Arabic text reads *la-waqaʿū-hā* [they would surely be moved to embrace her as a man embraces a woman] instead of *la-ẓannū anna-hum muwāqiʿū-hā* [they would surely suppose that they must be embracing her as a man embraces a woman]. The additional phrase at the end of the paragraph – about the impossibility of escape – occurs only in this second version of the report.

will say, as they cling to the Heavenly Throne [ʿ*Arsh*]: "My own soul, my own soul [*nafsī, nafsī*] – that is all I beg You to spare!"

Then Hell will send forth a shower of sparks, as numerous as the stars. Each spark will be like an enormous cloud arising in the West, and that shower of sparks will fall upon the heads of the assembled creatures.

This, then, is the shower of sparks [*sharar*] which Allāh will ward off from the true believers [*muʾminīn*] who faithfully discharge their solemn vow, and who are in dread of His chastisement, fearing that it might be inflicted upon them. For Allāh (Exalted is He) will surely protect all those who are committed to the affirmation of His Oneness and to faith [*ahl al-tawḥīd wa 'l-īmān*] – as He will protect all those who remain faithful to the example set by His Messenger [*ahl as-Sunna*] – from the evil [*sharr*] of that day.[34] He will cause them to experience His mercy. He will make their final reckoning easy for them to undergo. He will cause them to enter His Garden of Paradise, and He will grant them everlasting life therein, for all eternity, through His loving grace.

As for the unbelievers [*kāfirīn*], on the other hand, and those who are guilty of attributing partners to Him and of worshipping idols [*ahl ash-shirk wa 'l-awthān*], He will cause them to suffer evil upon evil, fear upon fear, and torment upon torment. For He will cause them to enter Hell [*Jahannam*], and He will make them live therein forever, for all eternity.

Then He has told us (Almighty and Glorious is He):

> *wa laqqā-hum naḍratan wa surūrā.*
> **And He has made them find cheerfulness and joy. (76:11)**

---

34 For a full understanding of the commentary devoted by the author (may Allāh be well pleased with him) to the Qur'ānic verse [*āya*]: *fa-waqā-humu 'llāhu sharra dhālika 'l-yawmi.* **Allāh has therefore warded off from them the evil of the day. (76:11)**, it ts important to be aware that the Arabic word *sharar* [(a shower of) sparks] is derived from the same triconsonantal root *SH-R-R* as the word *sharr* [evil].

Cheerfulness [*naḍra*] shows in people's faces,[35] while joy [*surūr*] is felt within their hearts.[36] What is alluded to here is the following experience:

As soon as the true believer [*muʾmin*] has emerged from his grave or tomb on the Day of Resurrection [*Yawm al-Qiyāma*], he will look straight ahead of himself. There, lo and behold, he will see a human being whose face is like the sun, and who is laughing merrily. This person will be dressed in white robes, and on his head there will be a crown.

The newly resurrected believer will gaze at the unusual individual, until the latter draws near to him and says: "Peace be upon you, O saintly friend of Allāh [*salāmun ʿalaik, yā waliyya 'llāh*]!" He will respond to this greeting by saying: "And upon you be peace [*wa ʿalaika 's-salām*]! Who are you, O servant of Allāh? Are you one of the angels [*malʾak mina 'l-malāʾika*]?" To this the other will reply: "No, by Allāh!" The following questions and answers will then be exchanged between the pair:

> "Are you one of the Prophets [*nabī mina 'l-anbiyāʾ*]?"
> "No, by Allāh!"
> "Are you one of those drawn near [to the Lord] [*mina 'l-muqarrabīn*]?"
> "No, by Allāh!"
> "Well then, who are you?"
> "I am your own righteous conduct [*ʿamal ṣāliḥ*]. I have come to greet you with the good news of your admission to the Garden of Paradise and salvation from the Fire of Hell."

---

35 The word *naḍra* [cheerfulness; cheerful radiance] also occurs in one other verse [*āya*] of the Qurʾān, where the context clearly confirms this comment by the author (may Allāh be well pleased with him):
taʿrifu fī wujūhi-him naḍrata 'n-naʿīm.
You will recognise in their faces the cheerful radiance of bliss. (83:24)
In its fullest sense, according to the classical Arabic lexicographers, the expression *naḍrata 'n-naʿīm* signifies "the beauty and brightness of aspect characteristic of blissful enjoyment" or "of a plentiful and pleasant and easy state of existence" or "the brightness, or glistening, and moisture upon the skin that is characteristic thereof." (See E.W. Lane, *Arabic-English Lexicon*, art. *N-D-R*)

36 It is significant to note that the word *surūr* [joy, happiness, gladness] is derived from the same triconsonantal root *S-R-R* as the term *sirr* [secret; the hidden recesses of the innermost being].

"O servant of Allāh, do you really know that for a fact, so that you can confidently give me such glad tidings?"
"Yes!"

Once this assurance has been given, the conversation will continue as follows:

"Well then, what do you want from me?"
"Climb up on my shoulders and use me as your means of transport."
"Glory be to Allāh [*Subḥāna 'llāh*]! It cannot be right and proper for the likes of you to be ridden as a means of transport!"
"Oh yes, it is entirely appropriate, considering how long I rode about on your shoulders in the realm of the lower world. So now I am begging you, for the sake of Allāh's countenance, to mount up and ride upon me."

The newly resurrected believer will thereupon agree to mount and ride upon the embodiment of his own righteous conduct, at which point the latter will say to him: "Do not be afraid! I shall be your escort to the Garden of Paradise."

This will make him feel happy, and his happiness [*faraḥ*] will become apparent in his face, so much so that it will soon be glistening and sparkling with delight. Radiant light [*nūr*] will be visible in his face, while joy [*surūr*] is felt within his heart, for this is in accordance with the words of Allāh (Almighty and Glorious is He):

wa laqqā-hum naḍratan wa surūrā.
And He has made them find cheerfulness and joy. (76:11)

As far as the unbeliever [*kāfir*] is concerned, as soon as he has emerged from his grave or tomb, he will also look straight ahead of himself. There, lo and behold, he will see a swarthy, blue-eyed man with an ugly face, swarthier than the pitch blackness of the tomb on a dark and gloomy night.

The man will be dressed in black robes. His canine teeth will scratch the ground, and, as he treads upon it, his footsteps will produce a rumbling noise like thunder. The stench he gives off will be worse than that of a rotting corpse.

The unbeliever, though wishing he could turn his face away from him, will say: "Who are you, O servant of Allāh?" To this the ugly figure will reply: "O enemy of Allāh, come here to me, come here to me! You belong to me, and I belong to you this day." The following exchanges will then take place between the pair:

> "Woe unto you! Are you a devil [*shaiṭān*]?"
> "No, by Allāh, but I am your own wicked conduct [*ʿamal ṭāliḥ*]!"
> "Well then, what do you want from me?"
> "I propose to mount upon your shoulders and use you as my means of transport!"
> "I implore you, by Allāh, to grant me a bit of leeway here, since you would be exposing me to disgrace in the sight of all my fellow creatures!"
> "By Allāh, there is no way out of your predicament, considering how long you rode about on me [in the realm of the lower world], so today I am going to mount up and ride upon you!"

The embodiment of his wicked conduct [*ʿamal ṭāliḥ*] will thereupon proceed to use the newly resurrected unbeliever as his means of transport, for this is in accordance with the words of Allāh (Almighty and Glorious is He):

> *wa hum yaḥmilūna awzāra-hum ʿalā ẓuhūri-him: a-lā sāʾa mā yazirūn.*
> **And they shall be carrying their burdens on their backs. O how evil are the loads they have to bear! (6:31)**

Then Allāh (Almighty and Glorious is He) has made mention of His saintly friends [*awliyā'*], for He has told us:

wa jazā-hum

And He has granted them, as a reward (76:12)

That is to say, in addition to the good tidings [of cheerfulness and joy].

bi-mā ṣabarū

for all that they have endured, (76:12)

That is to say, for their patient endurance in the face of trials and tribulations, in the performance of commandments and the avoidance of prohibitions, and in submissive acceptance of the decree of destiny [*qadar*].

jannatan wa ḥarīrā.

a Garden [of Paradise] and silk [attire]. (76:12)

As far as the Garden of Paradise is concerned, they will lead a life of ease and comfort therein. As for the silk, they will use it as the material for the clothes they wear.

Next, Allāh (Almighty and Glorious is He) has told us:

muttaki'īna fī-hā

[They will be] reclining therein... (76:13)

That is to say, in the Garden of Paradise.

'alā 'l-arā'ik.

upon [raised and canopied] couches. (76:13)

That is to say, upon raised couches [*surur*] with canopies [*ḥijāl*], i.e., curtains [*sutūr*], draped over them.[37]

> *lā yarawna fī-hā shamsan wa lā zamharīrā.*
> **They will experience there neither a sun nor bitter cold. (76:13)**

That is to say, they will not be afflicted by the heat of the sun, nor by the bitter cold of severe frost, because there is neither winter nor summer in the Garden of Paradise.

Then Allāh (Almighty and Glorious is He) has told us:

> *wa dāniyatan ʿalai-him ẓilālu-hā: wa dhullilat quṭūfu-hā tadhlīlā.*
> **And close upon them is the shade thereof, while its clustered fruits bow down low. (76:14)**

That is to say, the shade of the trees [is close upon them]. What is alluded to here is the following state of affairs:

The inhabitants of the Garden of Paradise may eat of its fruits while they are standing up, if they so wish, or while they are sitting down, if they so wish, or even, if they so wish, while they are sleeping. Whenever they want to enjoy some fruit, the clusters will bow down close enough to them for one of them to stand up and take his pick. Such is the explanation of His words (Almighty and Glorious is He):

> *wa dhullilat quṭūfu-hā tadhlīlā.*
> **while its cluster fruits bow down low. (76:14)**

---

37 According to the classical Arabic lexicographers, the term *arīka* (of which *arāʾik* is the plural form) denotes: "A raised couch [*sarīr*] in a *ḥajala*, which is a tent, or pavilion, or chamber, adorned with cloths or curtains." According to one authority, the *arīka* is so named because it was originally made of the wood of the thorny trees termed *arāk*, from which the sticks traditionally used for cleaning the teeth are also made. (See E.W. Lane, *Arabic-English Lexicon*, art. *ʾ-R-K*)

Then He has told us (Almighty and Glorious is He):

> *wa yuṭāfu ʿalai-him bi-āniyatin min fiḍḍatin wa akwābin.*
>
> **And flasks of silver are brought around for them, and vessels. (76:15)**

These vessels [*akwāb*] are actually mugs or tankards *[kīzān],* except that they have round tops[38] and are not equipped with handles. He has also said (Almighty and Glorious is He):

> *kānat qawārīrā qawārīran min fiḍḍatin.*
>
> **[Those vessels] are crystal beakers, crystal beakers made of silver. (76:15-16)**

In other words, the vessels concerned are of the type called *qawārīr* [beakers normally made of crystal, in the sense of clear, colourless glass of the highest quality], but in this case they are made of silver. The explanation of the seeming paradox is simply this: Whereas the *qawārīr* of this lower world are made of earthly material, the *qawārīr* of the Garden of Paradise are made of silver.

Allāh (Almighty and Glorious is He) has then added these words to His description of the vessels:

> *qaddarū-hā taqdīrā.*
>
> **They have measured them in exact proportion. (76:16)**

That is to say, the vessels [*akwāb*] have been measured to match the proportions of the flask [*inā'*], and the flask has been measured to fit the palm of the servant in charge of dispensing the people's drink. This has been done to ensure that exactly the right amount is always poured. Not a drop will be left in the flask, and not a drop too much will be poured, since

---

38 The roundness of their tops is referred to as a way of indicating that these vessels [*akwāb*] have no spouts. (See E.W. Lane, *Arabic-English Lexicon,* art. *K-W-B* and art. *K-W-Z*)

all the elements involved have been measured to correspond exactly. Such is the import of His words (Exalted is He):

qaddarū-hā taqdīrā.

They have measured them in exact proportion. (76:16)

He has also told us (Exalted is He):

wa yusqawna fī-hā kaʾsan.

And in it their thirst is quenched with a cup. (76:17)

That is to say, their thirst is quenched with a [cup of] wine [*khamr*], since no receptacle that does not contain wine can be called a cup [*kaʾs*]![39]

He has also told us (Exalted is He):

kāna mizāju-hā zanjabīlā.

The mixture of it is ginger. (76:17)

That is to say, the whole of it has had ginger [*zanjabīl*] mixed in with it. Then Allāh (Almighty and Glorious is He) has spoken of:

ʿainan fī-hā tusammā Salsabīlā.

A fountain therein, named *Salsabīl*. (76:18)

This fountain flows towards them from the Garden of Eden [*Jannat ʿAdn*][40] for it passes through every Garden, then returns to its source. It touches every part of the Garden of Paradise. He has also told us (Exalted is He):

wa yaṭūfu ʿalai-him wildānun mukhalladūn.

And waiting on them are immortal youths. (76:19)

---

39 According to the classical Arabic lexicographers, the term *kaʾs,* which usually means "a drinking-cup; a cup containing wine; a cup full of wine," may sometimes signify "wine" itself. When a cup does not contain wine, however, it is called *qadaḥ* instead of *kaʾs.* (See E.W. Lane, *Arabic-English Lexicon,* art. *K-ʾ-S*)

40 That is to say, according to the Arabic lexicographers, "the Garden of Perpetual Abode." (See E.W. Lane, *Arabic-English Lexicon,* art. *ʿ-D-N*)

These youths are the attendants [*ghilmān*] who will never become white-haired with age. Since they have been granted immortal youth, they will never attain the age of puberty, let alone grow old. Speaking of these ever-youthful attendants, Allāh (Almighty and Glorious is He) has told us:

> *idhā ra'aita-hum ḥasibta-hum lu'lu'an manthūrā.*
> **If you could see them, you would take for scattered pearls. (76:19)**

That is to say, they would seem like pearls on account of their handsome appearance and the whiteness of their complexion, and like scattered pearls on account of their great number. In other words, they would seem like scattered pearls too numerous for anyone to count them all.

Then Allāh (Almighty and Glorious is He) has told us:

> *wa idhā ra'aita thamma*
> **And when you see, there... (76:20)**

That is to say, over there in the Garden of Paradise.

> *ra'aita na'īmān wa mulkan kabīrā.*
> **You will see a state of bliss and a vast estate. (76:20)**

What this signifies in detail is as follows: Any man, who is numbered among the inhabitants of the Garden of Paradise, will be the owner of a palace. Within that palace there will be seventy palatial mansions. Inside every mansion there will be seventy apartments. Every apartment will be constructed from a hollowed pearl, the height of which extends skyward to the distance of a league [*farsakh*], while its width and length are a league by a league. It will be equipped with four thousand door panels made of gold.

Inside that apartment there will be a throne-like raised couch [*sarīr*], embroidered with threads of pearl and sapphire on the right side and the left, respectively. There will also be four thousand footstools made of gold, with supporting legs of red ruby. That throne-like raised couch will have seventy cushions spread upon its surface, every cushion of a different colour. The owner will be reclining there on his left side, clad in seventy articles of clothing tailored from silk brocade. The garment closest to his body will be made of white silk, and on his forehead he will wear a diadem [*iklīl*], embedded with chrysolite or peridot [*zabarjad*], sapphires, and various kinds of jewels, every jewel being of a different colour. Upon his head he will wear a crown of gold, with seventy corners to it, and on every corner a pearl as wide as the entire distance between the East and the West. On his wrist he will carry three bracelets: a bracelet of gold, a bracelet of silver, and a bracelet of pearl. On his fingers and toes he will be wearing rings of gold and silver, studded with various kinds of precious stones.

On duty in his presence there will be ten thousand ever-youthful attendants, who will never reach adulthood, let alone become white-haired with age.

A table made from a single red ruby will also be set in front of him, the size of its top being a mile in width by a mile in length. Laid out upon that table will be seventy thousand kitchen utensils made of gold and silver, and in each of those bowls and dishes there will be no fewer than seventy different kinds of food. Then, as soon as he has picked out some tasty morsel with his hand, it may occur to him that he would actually prefer another, in which case the taste and texture of the morsel concerned will immediately be transformed, so that it turns into the one he really fancies.

Youthful attendants [*ghilmān*] will be ready to wait upon him at table, holding drinking vessels of silver in their hands, as well as flasks of silver from which to pour his drink. They will have both wine and water with them. He will thus be able to eat as much of all the various dishes as forty men could ordinarily consume, for as soon as he has had his fill of a particular kind of food, they will give him a draught of whichever drink he happens to prefer, and he will then relieve his indigestion by burping and belching.

Allāh (Almighty and Glorious is He) will grant him access to a thousand different ways of experiencing an appetite.[41] The man will go on drinking till he breaks out in a sweat, then, once he has started to perspire, Allāh will make him aware of the existence of a thousand separate entrances to the appetite for food and drink. Through those entrances, birds resembling enormous thoroughbred she-camels will fly into his presence, alighting to form a row in front of him. Each bird will then proceed to offer a description of itself, in a charmingly melodious voice, more delightful by far than any singing to be heard in this lower world. It will say: "O saintly friend of Allāh [*yā waliyya 'llāh*], eat me up, for I have been raised and cared for in such and such an aviary in the pastures of the Garden of Paradise, and I am accustomed to drinking from such and such a fountain." The birds will go on appealing to him in those beautiful voices of theirs, until he eventually looks up and fixes his gaze on one bird in particular – the one with the most compelling voice, as well as the most attractive self-description – and feels the desire to make a meal of it. Allāh (Almighty and Glorious is He) is well aware, of course, of the liking for it that has now become lodged in the heart of His servant. That bird will therefore come at once and alight upon the table – part of it cut into strips, salted and dried [*qadīd*], part of it broiled, grilled or roasted [*shawi*], and all of it whiter than snow and sweeter than honey. The man will then proceed to eat until he has had his fill of it, until his appetite has been fully satisfied. At this point the bird will become a bird again, just as it was before, and it will fly out through the very door by which it entered.

---

41 Literally, "Allāh (Almighty and Glorious is He) will open up [*yaftaḥu*] for him a thousand doors or gates of appetite." The verb *yaftaḥu* is derived from the trilateral root *F-T-Ḥ*, which conveys the basic idea of "openness". For a full account of many important ramifications of this Arabic root, see the Translator's Introduction to *The Sublime Revelation* [*al-Fatḥ ar-Rabbānī*], another volume in the Al-Baz series of English translations of the works of Shaikh ʿAbd al-Qādir al-Jīlānī (may Allāh be well pleased with him).

As for the man, he will be reclining all the while "upon raised and canopied couches [*ʿalā ʾl-arāʾiki*],"[42] and his wife will be right there beside him, turning her face towards his. He will see his own face reflected in hers, on account of the pure clarity and whiteness of her complexion. Whenever he wishes to have sexual intercourse with her, he will give her a longing look, yet he will feel too shy to invite her in explicit terms.

She will be well aware, however, of what her husband wants from her, so she will make him a frank proposal, saying: "By my father and my mother, I urge you to raise your head and look at me directly, for you belong to me this day, and I belong to you!" He will respond to this by making love to her with all the strength and vigour of a hundred ancient heroes [*miʾa rajul min al-awwalīn*], and with all the passionate desire of forty stalwart men. When he approaches her sexually, he will discover that she is a virgin. He will not let his attention stray from her for one moment, during a period of forty days. Then, when he finally reaches the point of exhaustion, he will notice that the aroma of musk is emanating from her, and this will serve to increase still further the love he feels for her as a wife. As an inhabitant of the Garden of Paradise, he will have four thousand and eighty wives like her, and each wife will have seventy menservants and maidservants.

From another traditional report, this one transmitted on the authority of ʿAlī ibn Abī Ṭālib (may Allāh be well pleased with him), we learn that the Prophet (Allāh bless him and give him peace) once said:

> If a maidservant or a manservant [belonging to the inhabitants of the Garden of Paradise] were ever to emerge into this lower world, all the people of this world would surely engage in mortal combat over her or him, until they were all extinct. And if the maidens of Paradise, with eyes so fair [*al-ḥūr al-ʿīn*], were ever to let their locks

42 An allusion to the verse [*āya*] of the Qurʾān (76:13) discussed by the author (may Allāh be well pleased with him) on page 98 above. (See also note 37 above).

> of hair trail down upon the earth, the light of the sun would be extinguished, because of their vastly brighter radiance.

Someone once asked: "O Messenger of Allāh, how great is the contrast [in the Garden of Paradise] between the manservant [*khādim*], on the one hand, and the man who is served as a master [*makhdūm*], on the other?" To this he replied (Allāh bless him and give him peace):

> By the One in whose Hand my soul is held, the distinction [in the Garden of Paradise] between the manservant [*khādim*], on the one hand, and the man who is served as a master [*makhdūm*], on the other, is like the stars that are almost too faint to be visible, in contrast to the moon at the halfway point [i.e., in the middle of the month, when it is at the full].[43]

Let us now resume our description of the state of bliss enjoyed by that inhabitant of the Garden of Paradise:

> While he is sitting there upon his throne-like couch [*sarīr*], lo and behold, Allāh (Almighty and Glorious is He) will send him an angel, bearing seventy fine articles of clothing, each of a different kind. These gifts will be tucked out of sight between the two fingers of the angel, who will also be conveying the salutation of peace and contentment. On reaching the door of the man's abode, the angel will come to a halt, saying to the doorkeeper: "Permit me to enter the presence of Allāh's saintly friend [*walī*], for I come to him as the Messenger of the Lord of All the Worlds." The doorkeeper will say in

---

43 From the general context of this passage, it seems safe to assume that the contrast referred to here – first by the anonymous questioner and then by the Prophet (Allāh bless him and give him peace) – is one that exists in the Garden of Paradise, although this is not explicitly stated in either case. To confirm the assumption, we may adduce the rather similar traditional report (cited on page 85 above) from which we learn, on the authority of Abū Huraira (may Allāh be well pleased with him), that the Prophet (Allāh bless him and give him peace) also used to say: The handsomeness of the true specimen of manhood [*rajul*], in contrast to the handsomeness of the manservant [*khādim*] among the people of the Garden of Paradise, is like [the brilliance of] the moon on the night when it is full, in contrast to [the fainter brilliance of] the stars.

response: "By Allāh, I do not possess the authority to converse with him directly. Nevertheless, I shall mention you to my immediate superiors among the doorkeeping staff."

They will then refer the matter from one to another in turn, until the information finally reaches him, after passing through seventy doors. The last in the chain of doorkeepers will tell him: "O saintly friend of Allāh [*yā waliyya 'llāh*], the Messenger of the Lord of All the Worlds is waiting at the outside door." He will then grant permission for the messenger to enter into his presence, so the angel will come inside and say: "Peace be upon you, O saintly friend of Allāh [*as-salāmu ʿalaik, yā waliyya 'llāh*]! The Lord of Might and Glory (Almighty and Majestic is He) extends to you the greeting of peace, and He is well-pleased with you." On hearing this news, but for the fact that Allāh (Almighty and Glorious is He) has not condemned him to death, the man would die of sheer happiness. Such is the import of His words (Exalted is He):

> *wa riḍwānun mina 'llāhi akbar: dhālika huwa 'l-fawzu 'l-ʿaẓīm.*
> **And greater yet [is the promise of] good pleasure from Allāh; that is the mighty triumph. (9:72)**

Such is likewise the import of His words (Exalted is He):

> *wa idhā raʾaita.*
> **And when you see. (76:21)**

By this He means: "And when you, O Muḥammad, see."

> *thamma raʾaita naʿīman...*
> **There you will see a state of bliss... (76:21)**

That is to say, over there you will see the state of bliss in which he finds himself.

wa mulkan kabīrā.
and a high estate. (76:21)

He must be endowed with a high estate indeed, when the Messenger of Allāh, the Lord of All the Worlds, may not enter his presence without permission! Then Allāh (Glorious and Exalted is He) has told us:

ʿaliya-hum thiyābu sundusin khuḍrun wa istabraq.
Upon them will be green garments of fine silk and thick brocade. (76:21)

That is to say, their outer garments will consist of silk brocade [*dībāj*].[44] By using the expression "upon them [*ʿāliya-hum*]," He has simply allowed for the unstated but obvious fact that the undergarment, the one right next to the person's skin, will consist of plain white silk.[45]

Then He has told us (Exalted is He):

wa ḥullū asāwira min fiḍḍa.
They will also be adorned with bracelets of silver. (76:21)

In another verse [*āya*] from a different chapter [*sūra*] of the Qurʾān, we also read:

yuḥallawna fī-hā min asāwira min dhahabin wa luʾluʾā.
They will be adorned therein with bracelets of gold and of pearls. (22:23)

44 According to the classical Arabic lexicographers, the term *istabraq* is properly applied to thick *dībāj* [silk brocade], or, more precisely, to "closely woven, thick, beautiful *dībāj* [silk brocade] interwoven with gold." (See E.W. Lane, *Arabic-English Lexicon*, art. *D-B-J*)

45 In the context of the English translation alone, the expression "upon them" would hardly call for an explanation. In the original Arabic, however, the expression *ʿāliya-hum,* as a quite uncommon synonym for the familiar *ʿalai-him,* does seem to suggest a nuance in need of interpretation.

This means that there must be three types of bracelets altogether. Then Allāh (Almighty and Glorious is He) has told us:

> *wa saqā-hum Rabbu-hum sharāban ṭahūrā.*
>
> **And their Lord will slake their thirst with a pure drink. (76:21)**

In order to grasp the full significance of these words, one needs to be aware of the following scenario:

At the entrance to the Garden of Paradise there stands a tree, from whose trunk two fountains gush forth. So, whenever a man succeeds in crossing the Bridge over Hell [*aṣ-Ṣirāṭ*], and in reaching these two fountains, he will plunge into one of the springs in order to bathe himself therein. He will thus acquire an aroma that is even more delightful than musk. His physical height will now be seventy cubits [*dhirāʿ*], matching the stature of Adam (peace be upon him).[46]

All the people of the Garden of Paradise, the men and the women alike, will be of exactly the same age on the birthday of Jesus (peace be upon him), when each and every one of them will become a permanent thirty-three-year-old person. The young boy will grow older in a hurry, until he becomes a thirty-three-year-old adult, while the gray-haired elder will quickly shed his aged condition and revert to the age of thirty-three. All of them, the men and the women alike, will be endowed with the same good looks as Joseph, the son of Jacob (peace be upon them both).

As well as bathing himself in one of the two fountains, the man will drink from the other, thereby expelling all unworthy feelings from inside his breast, whether they be spite and malice, anxiety and worry, jealousy and

---

46 According to one traditional report, cited earlier in this Discourse (page 69 above), the physical height of Adam (peace be upon him) was sixty cubits rather than seventy.

envy, or grief and sorrow. For, by means of that water, Allāh (Almighty and Glorious is He) will bring his heart into the open. He will thus emerge with his heart in the same condition as the heart of Job [*Ayyūb*], and with his tongue transformed into one that can speak the Arabic language as fluently as the tongue of Muḥammad (may Allāh bless them both, and may He grant them peace).

The man and his companions will then press on beyond the two fountains, until they come to the gateway itself, at which point the guardians of the Garden of Paradise will say to them: "Have you been through the process of purification?" They will all say yes, so the guardians will say: "Enter, to dwell herein forever!" By greeting them with the good news of eternal residence, before the actual moment of entry [*bi 'l-khulūd qabla 'd-dukhūl*], they intend to assure them that they will never have to leave.

As soon as someone goes in through the entrance to the Garden of Paradise, he will be accompanied by the two angels who were always with him in the realm of the lower world, these being none other than the Noble Recorders [*al-Kirām al-Kātibīn*].[47] At that very same moment, lo and behold, he will notice the presence of another angel, this one accompanied by a thoroughbred she-camel, created from a single green corundum [*yāqūta khaḍrā'*]. Its bridle and reins appear to be made from a red ruby [*yāqūta ḥamrā'*]. As for the saddle on its back, the front and rear portions both consist of pearls and sapphires, while its main surface is of gold and silver. This angel will also bring with him seventy fine articles of clothing and other adornments [including a crown], so the man will try them on, as well as setting the crown upon his head.

47 These guardian angels are mentioned in the Qur'ān: *wa inna 'alai-kum la-ḥāfiẓīn: Kirāman Kātibīn ya'lamūna mā taf'alūn.* **And yet over you there are watchers, Noble Recorders, who know whatever you do. (82:10-12)** According to the traditional commentaries, every human being is constantly supervised by two of these guardian angels, one on the right to record the person's good deeds, and one on the left to record the bad deeds committed.

The angel, who will also be accompanied by ten thousand youthful attendants, resembling hidden pearls, will then say to the man: "O saintly friend of Allāh [*yā waliyya 'llāh*], you must mount up and ride, for this wondrous thoroughbred she-camel belongs to you, as do others just like her." He will thereupon adopt her as his means of transport, availing himself of the fact that she has a pair of wings, and that the range of her every stride extends to the farthest point in sight.

Riding along on the back of his fabulous thoroughbred she-camel, with ten thousand youthful attendants ever on duty in his presence, and still accompanied by the two angels who were always with him in this lower world, the man will now keep travelling until he reaches his palatial mansions, and makes himself at home in them.

Then Allāh (Glorious and Exalted is He) has told us [that it will be said unto them]:

inna hādhā kāna la-kum
"Behold, this...

In other words, all this that has been described for your benefit, in this form [*ṣūra*] and in this chapter [*sūra*] of the Qur'ān...[48]

jazā'an
is a reward for you.

48 From a linguist's point of view, it is interesting to note the decidedly unusual occurrence – directly side by side in the original Arabic sentence – of the two words *ṣūra* [form] and *sūra* [chapter of the Qur'ān]. (In the Arabic script, the difference in pronunciation – and consequently in meaning – is clearly indicated by spelling the former with the initial letter *ṣād*, and the latter with the initial letter *sīn*.)

That is to say, it is a reward for those deeds of yours that deserve to be well recompensed.

wa kāna saʿyu-kum...
And your endeavour [upon earth]...

That is to say, your work [*ʿamal*]...

mashkūrā.
has found acceptance." (76:22)

In other words, Allāh (Almighty and Glorious is He) has acknowledged the merit of your deeds, and He has therefore rewarded you with the Garden of Paradise.

[*al-ḥamdu li'llāhi Rabbi'l-ʿālamīn*]
Praise be to Allāh, the Lord of All the Worlds!